BRIGHT NOTES

THE AWAKENING BY KATE CHOPIN

Intelligent Education

Nashville, Tennessee

BRIGHT NOTES: The Awakening
www.BrightNotes.com

No part of this publication may be used or reproduced in any manner whatsoever without written permission, except in the case of brief quotations in critical articles and reviews. For permissions, contact Influence Publishers http://www.influencepublishers.com.

ISBN: 978-1-645422-98-3 (Paperback)
ISBN: 978-1-645422-99-0 (eBook)

Published in accordance with the U.S. Copyright Office Orphan Works and Mass Digitization report of the register of copyrights, June 2015.

Originally published by Monarch Press.
Nettie Litwak, 1987
2019 Edition published by Influence Publishers.

Interior design by Lapiz Digital Services. Cover Design by Thinkpen Designs.

Printed in the United States of America.

Library of Congress Cataloging-in-Publication Data forthcoming.
Names: Intelligent Education
Title: BRIGHT NOTES: The Awakening
Subject: STU004000 STUDY AIDS / Book Notes

CONTENTS

1)	Introduction to Kate Chopin	1
2)	Plot and Themes	6
3)	Chopin's Style and Symbolism	13
4)	Textual Analysis	
	Chapters 1–9	20
	Chapters 10–22	37
	Chapters 23–31	53
	Chapters 32–38	66
5)	Character Analysis	77
6)	Critical Reception of the Awakening	83
7)	Essay Questions and Answers	103
8)	Bibliography	109

INTRODUCTION TO KATE CHOPIN

BILINGUAL BACKGROUND

Born to an Irish father and a French mother, heir to two great literary traditions, Kate Chopin, whose maiden name was Katherine O'Flaherty, was born in 1851 and lived in St. Louis for the first twenty years of her life.

She was the only daughter of her father's second marriage to Eliza Faris, who was the daughter of a Huguenot father from Virginia, and a French mother from Missouri. Captain Thomas O'Flaherty was a successful businessman who became the director of the Pacific Railroad. Chopin's early childhood appears to have been very happy until her father was killed in a train wreck when she was only four. Thereafter, she was brought up in a household of strong women, all widows. Her matriarchal great-grandmother regaled the young Kate with wondrous stories, told in French, and the child grew up completely bilingual. A series of tragedies in the family were devastating to the child. She lost her brother, Thomas O'Flaherty, who drowned, and a beloved half-brother, George, in the Civil War, and mourned them for many years. One of Kate Chopin's daughters, describing her mother's personality, would say later that these early tragedies had left a "stamp of sadness on her that was never lost."

A LIBERATED HUSBAND - FOR HIS TIME

On a visit to the exciting city of New Orleans, Kate met her future husband, Oscar Chopin, who seems to have been an extraordinary man, for his time. He was a successful cotton broker, adored his wife for her independence and fine mind, and allowed her the sort of freedom that was rare in those days. Even on her honeymoon in Europe, Kate took solitary walks, always observing, watching people, noting settings, and actually, displaying all the attributes of a writer. The young couple spent three months in Germany, Switzerland, and France, and then returned to live in New Orleans, a city that seems to have fascinated Kate. She continued her solitary walks, observing the Creole society, the mixture of Cajun, Blacks, Mulattoes, Germans, Italian, Irish, who populated the city, and gave it an exotic flavor. She was particularly intrigued by the Blacks whose songs and racy French, patois filled with superstitious lore, stimulated her early writings. The climate of New Orleans gave the city a Southern European flavor and the foliage of jasmine and magnolia trees filled the city with sultry fragrance.

THE SETTING FOR THE AWAKENING

With her Irish ear for music and story, this city was a catalyst on the young woman's imagination, and laid the groundwork for her work as a local colorist. Summers spent on the islands off the coast of Louisiana gave Kate the setting for her controversial novel, *The Awakening*.

New Orleans had many cultural riches to offer a receptive young wife. Kate attended the Academy of Music, the two opera houses that the city boasted, the theaters. She was herself an accomplished pianist and knew and responded passionately to music. The local newspapers often included excerpts from the works of Flaubert, Gautier, Maupassant, Baudelaire, and since Kate was an avid reader, she became familiar with these great French writers.

The Chopins had six children. Kate is remembered as having been a loving and conscientious mother. Oscar Chopin began having troubles with his business, and in 1880, he was forced to move his family to Cloutierville, a Cajun area in western Louisiana. Her husband's misfortune turned out to be Kate's fortune, for it was here that she learned more about the Cajuns (descendants of French exiles from Acadia, now Nova Scotia), and began collecting the lore of a region that was strange, exotic, and relatively unknown to the rest of the country. The mixture of French, African, Spanish, and English spun a magic web that captured Kate's imagination and to which she responded with sympathetic understanding. During the yellow fever epidemic that took four thousand lives in New Orleans alone, Oscar Chopin died, leaving Kate a young widow with six small children. She was only thirty. For a year after her husband's death, she remained in Louisiana, tending her husband's business, but her mother wanted her to return to St. Louis, and so in 1884, she sold the business, and returned to the city of her birth. In June 1885, Kate's mother died suddenly, leaving her now all alone, except for her children.

URGED TO WRITE FICTION - AS THERAPY

A friend, Doctor Kolbenheyer, who had been her obstetrician and was now her family doctor, urged her to write fiction. He believed that her letters to him, written while she was living in Louisiana, had literary merit. In the hope that writing might help her overcome her depression at the loss of her husband,

and might even give her a little income, the doctor urged her to put down some of her impressions and memories of the years she had spent in Louisiana.

She wrote in the family living room, surrounded by her children, and only worked a few mornings a week. She was an avid card player, and once again began to attend the concerts, plays, and recitals that she had always enjoyed. In time, her home became a sort of French literary salon for distinguished women in St. Louis. Her "day" was Thursday.

Her first work in print was in a progressive Chicago magazine called *America* which published her poem titled, "If It Might Be," on January 16, 1889. Stories about Louisiana plantation life were published in the *St. Louis Post Dispatch* and in the *Philadelphia Musical Journal*. Her first novel, *At Fault*, probably published at the author's expense, did not sell well, but it foreshadowed Chopin's later writings, with its **theme** of individual freedom and what the desire for it can cost the person who wants it. After 189, she began to sell to magazines like *Century, Youth's Companion*, and *Vogue*. Her reputation developed as a regional writer of local color and with the publication of *Bayou Folk* and *A Night in Acadie*, she became very well regarded as an exquisite writer of minor tales.

OSTRACIZED FROM POLITE SOCIETY

When *The Awakening* was published in 1899, the critics were shocked and scandalized by the story of a woman who is passionately awakened by her senses, who leaves her husband's home, is uninterested in her children, who has an affair, and who desperately wants freedom for herself, refusing to accept the conventional role of wife, mother, society matron, adornment to her husband's position. Kate Chopin was thereafter reviled and ostracized by polite society in St. Louis. Broken-hearted, Chopin wrote very little after this, and died in 1904.

THE AWAKENING

PLOT AND THEMES

PLOT

The story unfolds gradually in two distinct settings: Grand Isle and New Orleans. Carefully structured to reveal Edna Pontellier's gradual awakening to a true understanding of her own nature, the story is told chronologically from Edna's stay at the summer resort on Grand Isle, to her return after the summer to her elegant home in New Orleans, and to her eventual return to Grand Isle where she makes her final decision.

Only one chapter takes us back to Edna's childhood (chapter 7), when Edna confides in her friend, Adele Ratignolle, allowing the reader some insight into the character's background; all the rest of the action moves mainly straight ahead, inexorably, to the end.

A series of events takes place in Edna's life that move the action along, rather leisurely at first, as befits a story taking place in a relaxed summer resort, then picking up speed when she returns to the more hectic tempo of the city of New Orleans, and ending with her return to Grand Isle.

Edna's flirtation with Robert Lebrun; her difficulties in her marriage and with her children; her sensual response to the exotic surroundings of Grand Isle; her oppression at church services; her shedding of clothing; her mastery of swimming; her response to music; her reluctant return to her duties in New Orleans; her growing friendship with Mademoiselle Reisz, an independent woman; her disappointment with Robert Lebrun; her sexual attraction to Alcee Arobin; her decision to move out of her husband's house; her return to Grand Isle; are the plot developments that serve to build an accretion of detail that move the story to its culmination. Chopin shows great economy in her choice of plot events; they all serve her purpose: to show how Edna Pontellier awoke and what happened after she did.

THEMES

Escape theme

From the opening screech of the caged parrot outside a pension on the island of Grand Isle, a resort off the coast of Louisiana, the **theme** of escape from maternal and matrimonial bondage is heard. "Get out! Get out!" screams the parrot, and that is just what Edna Pontellier tries to do.

The constrictions of marriage

Leonce Pontellier is not a brute, and Edna's life is actually a luxurious one, free from the brutalization of poverty. But at this time (the 1800s) and in this place (Creole society in New Orleans), a woman is severely restricted. Marriage brings with it certain obligations: to husband, to society, to children, to others. Fulfilling one's own needs is not part of a married woman's life. She must subjugate herself to her husband and to her family. The husband is much freer. He, of course, works, but that more or less relieves him of the responsibilities of home and family. Although Edna did not have to personally do the cooking, cleaning and so on, it was her responsibility to see that the servants did all the necessary work to maintain the establishment. Edna had to entertain a certain way; she had a day in which she received acquaintances. She had to look a certain way; her husband valued appearances. She was supposed to be skilled in music, art, literature, but not too skilled. Her life was to be devoted to her family. Once Edna realizes how unfulfilling this is to her true nature, she begins to rebel and to try and "get out!"

Constrictions of motherhood

Edna's two little boys are not clearly characterized. They are just children; interchangeable. We hardly can see any difference between Raoul and Etienne Pontellier. Significantly, they do not cling to Edna; they do not run to her when they are hurt. But they always need something - food, treats, games, time. They get sick; they fall down and hurt themselves. Their needs are constant and demanding. A mother must nurture her children before herself. Edna is not a "mother-woman," like the other women on the island. She does not immerse herself in maternity. In fact, she is relieved when the children go to visit their paternal grandmother and she gets some time away from their interminable demands. Motherhood, for Edna, is not the exhilarating experience it is for other women. To her, children are a trap.

The constrictions of society

Edna must summer on the island where the other members of the wealthy Creole society stay. She feels like an outsider there, and probably would have preferred another kind of vacation. It seems that she is never consulted. She must go where her husband's friends and associates go. In addition to spending time with people she is not very comfortable with, Edna also has a "day" during which she must entertain. This is what people in this stratum of society do. When she rebels, and refuses to continue doing this, her husband is shocked. He suspects that she is mentally ill. One must look, dress, speak a certain way in this society. Edna cannot and will not conform. She engages in a flirtation with Robert Lebrun, the resort owner's son, and makes the mistake of taking it more seriously than she should. In this society, such a flirtation is not serious. Edna should have followed the rules; she doesn't. She also makes the mistake of allowing another man, Alcee Arobin, known by everyone to be a rouge, to make love to her. This behavior is not countenanced by society.

The pain of rebellion

Edna rebels, but at enormous cost, actually, the ultimate cost, her life. Once she realizes the truth of her own nature, that she is a passionate, sensual woman, who will probably have many affairs, who is not content with her husband, and whose children do not fill all her needs, Edna knows that she cannot continue to live the way she has in the past. She cannot reconcile her own desires with that of her husband and children, and so she ends her own life.

The importance of one's own identity

Confiding to Adele Ratignolle, the epitome of the "mother-woman," Edna says that although she would give her life for her children, she will not give herself. Adele, of course, is shocked by this blasphemy and probably doesn't even understand what Edna is talking about, but Edna knows what she is saying. Children, for Edna, are a constant pulling on her own selfhood. To give herself up to her children means losing herself. This, she says, she cannot do. She is willing to sacrifice everything in order to be a person herself, and not just an appendage, no matter how ornamental.

The danger of passion

Robert Lebrun's teasing tantalizes Edna. She begins to be very aware of his person, to miss him when he is away, and is devastated when he finally goes to Mexico, as he has promised to do for a long time. She becomes more infatuated with Robert but allows herself to be seduced by Alcee Arobin. When she realizes that, perhaps, what she was pretending was a grand passion for Robert is only a sexual desire that can be satisfied by Alcee, she begins to understand her own nature, and the danger of passion. She says, at one point, that she married her husband because she knew that passion would not intrude and spoil the gentle affection she feels for him. Edna has always regarded passion as dangerous, even before her marriage to Leonce. She must have had some understanding of her susceptibility, even as a girl. Edna pays for her passion with her life.

The danger of art and music

Music can excite the passions. When Edna hears Mademoiselle Reisz play the piano she is moved to tears. She cannot speak. The musician recognizes in Edna a great susceptibility to this kind of stimuli. Edna dabbles in art herself, but she is a dilettante;

she does not have the discipline to be a great artist. She also understands how demanding art is, how it must exclude other considerations. Leonce regards Edna's sketching with somewhat patronizing amusement, but when she appears to become serious about her work, he is very upset. This "amusement" is causing disharmony in his household. Edna is not acting like a good wife and mother. Art and its demands are distracting her from her primary job.

The sleeping beauty theme

Edna spends a great deal of time sleeping. Even on an expedition with Robert, the man she is infatuated with, she gets so drowsy that she has to go to sleep in Madame Antoine's house. She sleeps for a long time, awakens, and asks Robert how long she has been sleeping. He tells her she has slept for a hundred years. In the fairy tale, the sleeping princess is awakened by a kiss, to love. In *The Awakening*, Edna awakens to hunger for food. She eagerly eats, savoring the simple fare provided to her. She seems to have awakened to her physical desires. Once awakened, she can never be the same again.

The danger of awakening

Kate Chopin called her novel, *The Awakening* even though she had chosen another name for it first: *A Solitary Soul*. This original title had the theme of alienation, difference from others, and anguish. The title was changed to *The Awakening*, but the **themes** remain. Once Edna becomes aware of certain things in herself that she would have liked, perhaps, to have kept repressed, she can no longer continue living the life she did before. There is danger in waking up. There is danger in being alienated from others, in being different. It is far safer to be like everyone else. Edna, now fully awake, can no longer go back to sleep.

The journey

Edna's journey to self-knowledge is very painful. She must first recognize and admit what, to a woman at this time, must have been shocking: she is a sexual being. She must bring herself to acknowledge that she is not a "mother-woman," and that she is different from all the other women she knows. She goes back and forth between Grand Isle and New Orleans, and she goes back and forth between self-knowledge and self-deceit. Honesty wins out, but she destroys herself. She cannot live at the end of her quest, and it is significant that her final act takes place at Grand Isle, the locale of her awakening. She ends her journey where she had begun it: in the sea.

THE AWAKENING

CHOPIN'S STYLE AND SYMBOLISM

STYLE

Chopin writes simply, with restraint and economy, especially for her era. She uses short sentences, short chapters; chapter 28 is just one page long (it is the chapter in which Edna finally understands herself). At times she can be poetic. Her descriptions of the sea are Whitmanesque, and she repeats some of the lines (chapter 6 and the final chapter) that emphasize the **theme**. She sprinkles French phrases throughout, establishing the particular flavor of her characters' speech. Chopin was trilingual and quite at home with Creole, French, and English.

POINT OF VIEW

She tells her story from the objective third-person point of view, but there is an occasional narrative intrusion by the author that colors our view of the characters and events. We begin to look forward to these wry, intelligent comments. The first chapter is written through Leonce Pontellier's point of view as he watches his wife approach under her pink-lined sunshade with Robert

Lebrun, the young man who is attentive to her. The rest of the book is told through Edna's point of view, with an occasional shift to Leonce's perspective.

Chopin is always respectful to her creations. She doesn't judge them; she understands them. "Mr. Pontellier had been a rather courteous husband so long as he met a certain tacit submissiveness in his wife." This kind of quiet aside certainly tells us a lot about this conventional Creole husband. Yet, Chopin doesn't dislike him, nor does she intend that we dislike him. "Robert talked a great deal about himself. He was very young and did not know any better." A narrative commentary on the self-centeredness of youth, but it is always kind.

DIALOGUE

Dialogue is used to establish character. In chapter 7, for example, where Edna is confiding, for the first time, in Adele Ratignolle, she tells Adele about her childhood. The first few pages of this chapter are in dialogue, which clearly shows Edna to be an unhappy, confused woman, repressed by her childhood memories, and unfulfilled in her marriage. In chapter 8, Adele asks Robert to stop flirting with Edna because she will make the mistake of taking him too seriously. This exchange is also rendered in dialogue and clearly establishes the nature of the relationship between these two characters. The dialogue itself is usually terse, interspersed with French and Creole expressions. The speaker is always easily identifiable without the author having to repeat the attributives, "he said," "she said."

SYMBOLISM

The lovers

Anonymous, seen in the background, completely immersed in each other, they have no names, little physical description to identify them. They are "lovers." Always together, always facing one another, silent, "They were leaning toward each other as the water oaks bent from the sea. There was not a particle of earth beneath their feet. Their heads might have been turned upside down, so absolutely did they tread upon blue ether." Obviously symbolic, not developed, these figures stand for the total absorption of people in love. To be in love like this means to sunder contact with others. These two are complete; they need no one else. It is the kind of relationship that Edna would like to have with Robert, a romantic ideal.

The lady in black

It is interesting to note that the lovers are always followed by the "lady in black." This is another one-dimensional character who functions symbolically. She is a religious figure, counting her rosary, reading from her prayer book. Her mourning clothes are symbolic of death and denial, of loss and grief. As a reminder of the oppressiveness of religion, and as a reminder of the death that eventually overcomes even lovers, she serves a double function in the novel. She reappears frequently as a reminder of our mortality. She is always seen in conjunction with the lovers. In a strange way, she may also function as a sort of chaperone.

Grand Isle

An Eden, a primitive, sensual island of warmth, of flowers, surrounded by the warm waters of the Gulf of Mexico, it is here that Edna eats the tree of knowledge, and is awakened to a full understanding of her own nature. The waters murmur ceaselessly; the breezes are balmy; a loosening of repressions occurs in this atmosphere. The island is a symbol of freedom, of paradise.

Madame Antoine's house

On the island of Cheniere Caminada, where Sunday mass is held, Madame Antoine's "cot" is immaculate, and a haven for a disturbed Edna. The oppression of the church service, perhaps the recollection of rules and **convention**, stifle Edna and she is taken to Madame Antoine's to recover from the atmosphere of the church. In the house, she removes part of her clothing, becomes aware for the first time of the texture of her own skin, sleeps for a long time, and awakens to a sensual repast of bread and wine (symbolic of the Catholic mass?) This place is a pleasant haven for Edna, but it is also a spot where she begins to savor taste - of food, of wine, of skin, of earthiness. The cot symbolizes a place removed from the ordinary, where a woman, moving away from conventional rules, can begin to indulge her own appetites. This island is a little removed from Grand Isle. Grand Isle is a paradise of innocence; Cheniere Caminada is an island where innocence is departing, leaving in its place appetite.

Nudity

Women in this period of time wore many layers of clothing: petticoats, drawers, corsets, long skirts, camisoles, gloves, hats. It is impossible to move freely, with abandon, trussed up like this. Edna removes the layers of her clothing gradually. In an intimate talk with Adele Ratignolle, when she confides in another human being for the first time, she removes her collar and opens her dress at the throat. It is the first symbol of her discarding of convention.

In Mme Antoine's house, on another island, Edna removes most of her clothing and awakens further to the feel of her own body. At the end of the book, back on Grand Isle, Edna removes all her clothing "and for the first time in her life she stood naked in the open air, at the mercy of the sun, the breezes that beat upon her, and the waves that invited her." The removal of all her clothing and her decision to swim far out, "where no woman had swum before," are symbols of her liberation from a life that would eventually constrict and destroy her. She chooses death, but it is her choice; in her ending is her freedom.

The pigeon house

Virginia Woolf, in her remarkable essay "A Room of One's Own", written years after *The Awakening* was published, said that in order to create art, one must have a "room of one's own." Women have not had this luxury. The room is, of course, symbolic of a place where one can quietly and privately nurture creativity. Women's first responsibility has been, not to themselves, but to others: children, husband, parents, community, society. Woolf said once women acquire this room and their own incomes, then they could become artists.

In 1899, Kate Chopin, the mother of six children, a widow after only twelve years of marriage, understood the need for a room all too well. Her character, Edna Pontellier, rebels against the constraints of her life, and tells her husband she is going to leave his home and move into a little house of her own, around the corner, which she calls "the pigeon house." The move out of her husband's sphere and influence is central to Edna's desire for independence. It is symbolic of her desire to be her own mistress, to live in her own home, to pay her own bills, to have space and time for herself and for her art, about which she has no great illusions.

Bird symbolism

The first screeching of the caged parrot, hung outside the pension on the island of Grand Isle, "Get out! Get out!" establishes the symbolism of a bird in a cage. Edna is a bird. Her cage is gilded; it is comfortable, but nevertheless, it confines her. Marriage and motherhood restrict Edna. She is described as having "quick, bright" eyes. There is something bird-like about her appearance. The cries of "Get out! Get out!" are heard again in the book. Although this symbolism is not particularly subtle, the recurrence is dramatic. In a conversation about art, the musician Mademoiselle Reisz puts her arms around Edna and feels her shoulder blades, to see if her wings are strong, for she says, "that the bird that would soar above the level plain of tradition and prejudice must have strong wings. It is a sad spectacle to see the weaklings bruised, exhausted, fluttering back to earth." Here again we see the image of a bird in relation to Edna.

When Edna moves out of her husband's house into a tiny place of her own, her new shelter is called "the pigeon house." Pigeons are not caged; they are free to come and go, unlike the parrot who has been tamed and domesticated. Edna views the pigeon house as a place where she can be free of her habitual constraints, and for the first time in her life exercise her independence.

The last example of bird **imagery** occurs at the end of the book where Edna sees "a bird with a broken wing … beating the air above, reeling, fluttering, circling disabled down, down to the water." Right after this, she enters the waters of the Gulf for the last time.

THE AWAKENING

TEXTUAL ANALYSIS

CHAPTERS 1-9

CHAPTER I

Bird symbolism and theme

A green and yellow parrot, hung in a cage outside the door of the main house on Grand Isle, an island fifty miles south of New Orleans, keeps repeating over and over, "Allez vous-en! Allez vous-en! Sapristi!" (Get out! Get out! Damn it!)

The parrot's command immediately establishes the **theme** of *The Awakening*. Edna Pontellier, the main character, who does not appear immediately in this opening chapter, will struggle to get out of her cage of marriage and motherhood. She will be damned for her struggles. The mockingbird's whistle echoes the sounds of the parrot, mocking, jeering.

Leonce Pontellier

A successful New Orleans broker, Leonce Pontellier's first action is one of impatience and even disgust. The parrot's sounds annoy him. He is restless, forty years old, of medium height, his beard is neatly trimmed. He gets up and moves away from the bird sounds. He does not want to hear them, just as he does not want to hear his wife's sounds.

Point of View

The author lets us see Edna Pontellier through her husband's eyes. He watches her, approaching under a white sunshade and chatting with Robert Lebrun, the son of the owner of the pension on Grand Isle. Leonce's first words. "You are burnt beyond recognition' .... looking at his wife as one looks at a valuable piece of personal property which has suffered some damage," show him to be a man to whom appearance is very important. His wife must take care of her looks. To get sunburned is unbecoming for a woman like Edna. She might be mistaken for a servant. This would be intolerable to Leonce. Edna is his property. One takes good care of valuable possessions. Throughout the book, Edna will struggle not to be anyone's property.

Marriage

The Pontellier marriage is strained. Edna prefers the company of Robert Lebrun to that of her husband. Leonce prefers the company of the New Orleans club men at Klein's Hotel, where he can play billiards. When Edna asks whether Leonce will return to dinner, he merely shrugs. She doesn't seem to care if he eats elsewhere. Both husband and wife are indifferent to each other.

Sounds to Establish Setting

The bird sounds, the sounds of the Farival twins playing a duet on the piano, Madame Lebrun's loud orders to her servants, the sound of her starched skirts crinkling, the sounds of the children at play, all establish a summer day of warmth and ease. The sound of Edna and Robert giggling together over some private nonsense bonds them together.

CHAPTER TWO

Edna's physical appearance

Edna's eyes, quick and bright, yellowish brown, have about them something of the parrot. "She was rather handsome than beautiful. Her face was captivating by reason of a certain frankness of expression and a contradictory subtle play of features. Her manner was engaging." Edna's appearance, the contradictory nature of her appeal, sets her apart from the other simpler women on the island.

Robert's physical appearance

He looks something like Edna. He is clean-shaven. "There rested no shadow of care upon his open countenance." The cigar he had in his pocket was given to him by Mr. Pontellier. He does not have a lot of money and speaks frequently of going to Mexico on business. (But he will not go until he becomes frightened by Edna's feelings for him.)

Shift in point of view

Although we first see Edna from her husband's point of view, in the second chapter the narrator's voice emerges when she comments on Edna and Robert's conversation. "Robert talked a great deal about himself. He was very young and did not know any better. Mrs. Pontellier talked a little about herself for the same reason." Authors can choose to use different points of view to tell their stories. They can use first person, which is a very limited point of view. Although we can empathize with a first-person narrator, the perspective is necessarily limited to what the "I" knows. Realizing these limitations, many authors choose to have a more flexible narrator. They decide on a third-person ("he," "she") point of view, which can be author omniscient (all-knowing), and can see and know what everyone is doing and thinking. An author also has the choice of using a limited third-person point of view. He can tell the story using "he," or "she," and we see what this one character sees and we feel what the one character feels. Chopin uses a third-person point of view. Most of the time we see Edna's point of view, but occasionally we are shifted to Leonce's point of view, and Chopin also avails herself the prerogative of authorial omniscient intrusions. She has given herself a great deal of flexibility in using these different perspectives.

Authorial intrusion

Chopin was writing in 1899. Readers were used to hear comments from the narrator. In fact, many discerning readers enjoyed these authorial intrusions as much as they enjoyed hearing the characters. The comments on both Edna and

Robert's youth are gently ironic, but kind. "He [Robert] was always intending to go to Mexico, but some way never got there," In chapter 2 we hear the author's voice for the first time. It is a voice we will come to like for its humor, its affection for the characters, with their failings, and for its steadfast intelligence.

Conversation to establish character

Left alone when Mr. Pontellier goes to Klein's Hotel, Edna and Robert reveal a lot about themselves through their conversation. Robert wants to go to Mexico, but somehow never gets there. He is concerned about the future. Edna talks about her father's Mississippi plantation and her home in the Old Kentucky Bluegrass Country. She talks about her sisters, her dead mother. She seems more interested in the past. There is a leisurely quality about the day and the conversation. It is holiday and summer and the talk is unhurried.

CHAPTER 3

Characterization

Leonce returns from Klein's Hotel at 11:00 that night in a very good mood. He disturbs his wife, who is already sleeping, talks to her even though she only murmurs in response. His actions show a man who is callous to his wife's needs, and utterly wrapped up in his own. He doesn't care about disturbing Edna. He is annoyed by her lack of response. This chapter starts once again with Leonce's point of view, and then shifts to Edna.

Irony

The narrator puts an unconsciously ironic thought into Leonce's head. "He thought it very discouraging that his wife, who was the sole object of his existence, evinced so little interest in things which concerned him, and valued so little his conversation." Our glimpses of Leonce, so far, hardly prepare us to think that Edna is "the sole object of his existence." The punning use of the word "object" once again emphasizes Edna's value to her husband as a possession, albeit a valuable one.

Marital conflict as theme

Leonce reproaches his wife for neglecting their children, yet he has forgotten to bring back the bonbons and peanuts that he had promised to the children. Edna refuses to answer her husband. After he goes to sleep, she goes out on the porch and weeps. She feels oppressed, but does not yet blame her husband. She laments her fate, but is still unawakened. "She was just having a good cry all to herself."

Sounds

The hooting of an owl, the sound of the sea, the buzzing of the mosquitoes, set the scene for this marital spat. Edna is finally driven indoors by the relentless insects. The sea sounds begin to make themselves heard in this chapter, a little louder than before. The sea is symbolic of Edna's gradual awakening.

Departure

Mr. Pontellier eagerly leaves Grand Isle the following morning for the city where he will stay until the following Saturday. Everyone, children, servants, ladies, gentlemen, come to say goodbye. He gives his wife half of the money that he had brought away from Klein's Hotel the previous evening.

Author's satiric comment

When Edna takes the money from her husband, the narrative voice comments gently, but satirically. "She liked money as well as most women." There is a wry quality to the commentary that we begin to expect and to look forward to.

Gifts that symbolize a marriage

A few days later, a box arrives for Mrs. Pontellier from her husband. It is filled with delicacies. Edna shares these gifts with the rest of the guests on the island. When everyone declares that Mr. Pontellier is the best husband in the world, "Mrs. Pontellier is forced to admit that she knew of none better." This statement, seemingly wrested from Edna's lips, says a great deal about her own husband, and about most husbands of Edna's acquaintance. The gifts look good, taste good, but are very trivial. They are also quickly gone, leaving the receiver with little. The marriages are the same: they look good to the outsider; they are beautifully packaged. Yet they are not substantial. Just like the gift boxes.

CHAPTER 4

Children

Edna's children, two little boys, do not rush to their mother's arms for comfort if they fall. They pick themselves up, they fight for themselves. Their nurse takes care of their physical needs. They seem surprisingly self-assured and independent, perhaps because of Edna's inability to be a "mother-woman." We see them always asking for something: food, attention. They are like children everywhere, but they are not developed as individuals. They are little animals who make enormous demands on a mother who doesn't derive great pleasure in filling their needs.

Mother-women

"They were women who idolized their children, worshipped their husbands, and esteemed it a holy privilege to efface themselves as individuals and grow wings as ministering angels." This commentary by the narrative voice, using words such as "idolized," "holy," "wings," "angels," is satiric in its use of religious **imagery**. In spite of the seeming praise, these "mother-women" do not seem admirable. They are excessive; their self-negation is a quality that neither Edna nor the narrator admire.

Adele Ratignolle-embodiment of the mother-woman

Adele looks like a romantic heroine with her spun-gold hair streaming unconfined, blue eyes like sapphires, exquisite hands that are always busy sewing a child's garment. She is always concerned with her children, but uses her constant pregnancies to get attention. Edna realizes this when Adele claims she is faint, but the color never fades from her face. Her conversation is all about her children. She is capable of showing great excitement about a pair of infant drawers. Edna cannot. Adele seems very comfortable with her role in life. She can speak about sex and pregnancies easily. Edna cannot.

Alienation

Edna is not a Creole, like the other guests on Grand Isle. Even though she lives among them, she feels uncomfortable around their "absence of prudery," combined at the same time with a "lofty chastity." When she is given a rather shocking book to read, she reads it in secret while the others read it openly.

Danger in books

Like Flaubert's Emma Bovary, who is stimulated and enchanted by romantic novels, Edna Pontellier is easily inflamed by literature. Both *The Awakening* and *Madame Bovary* share the **theme** that there is considerable danger in novels that can confuse susceptible weak women.

CHAPTER 5

Courtly love

In the Middle Ages many fine ladies had a courtly suitor. This knight would prostrate himself before his lady, kiss the hem of her gown, carry her favor into battle, idealize her. The relationship was not supposed to be sexual, a matter that is still open to conjecture. Robert Lebrun devotes himself to Edna in the manner of a courtly suitor. He fetches her shawl, drinks, and books. He is constantly in attendance. This is not the first time Robert has played the devoted swain. One summer he was very attentive to Adele Ratignolle, but she understood the game.

Hyperbole

Robert talks of his hopeless passion for Madame Ratignolle. He talks "of sleepless nights, of consuming flames till the very sea sizzled when he took his daily plunge." He assumes this serio-comic tone and Madame Ratignolle laughs at him. They both understand the rules of the game. Robert does not speak in this manner to Edna. Their game is a different one, even though it might look the same to the casual outsider. Edna, the alien, is not a Creole who is accustomed to passion; she is unfamiliar with the banter between a married woman and a single man that is part of the Creole tradition. It seems to be a mock courtly love and the rules are understood by the players. Edna, though, is not a player.

Edna's art

Edna dabbles in sketching. Yet "she felt in it satisfaction of a kind which no other employment afforded her." The other "mother-women" do not seek this kind of creativity. If they play the piano, as Adele does, they do it for the children, not for themselves. She sketches Madame Ratignolle, but is not satisfied with the portrait of her friend. It does not look like her. Does Edna see Adele as she really is, rather than the prettified version? She destroys the sketch. The narrator tells us that her sketching showed "natural aptitude, rather than many years of work." Edna has been a dilettante. She has never disciplined herself to hard, demanding work.

CHAPTER 6

Internal conflict

When Madame Ratignolle leaves Edna and Robert to go to her children, Robert asks Edna if she would like to bathe. Her first response is to say no. She doesn't quite understand this answer herself, and when she finally agrees, she realizes it was what she really wanted.

Sea symbolism

The waters of the Gulf are always seductive, "never ceasing, whispering, clamoring, murmuring, inviting the soul to wander for a spell in abysses of solitude; to lose itself in mazes of inward contemplation. The voice of the sea speaks to the soul. The touch of the sea is sensuous, enfolding the body in its soft, close embrace." Edna is beginning to awaken to the spell of the sea, and to feel her own sexual birth. "A certain light was beginning to dawn dimly within her." Robert's importuning, the sea sounds, her own sensuality begin to stir in her and she agrees to swim with Robert, at a time when the other women have gone into the cottages with their children. This extremely short chapter, just one page, is important. In it Edna takes the first step to her awakening. The prose poetry of the passages of the sea are very reminiscent of Walt Whitman's "Out of The Cradle Endlessly Rocking," published some forty years before Chopin wrote. The sea, for both authors, is both seductive and symbolic of rebirth.

CHAPTER 7

A study in contrasts

Edna Pontellier is described as reserved, with a noble beauty that is not readily apparent to the casual observer. Her body has long, clean lines, while Adele, although as tall, is more feminine. Adele has a fuller figure, is very careful of her complexion, and has to be persuaded by Edna not to bring her children along to the beach. She insists, though, in bringing her ever-present needlework.

Symbolism of setting

The road to the beach consists of "a long, sandy path, upon which a sporadic and tangled growth that bordered it on either side made frequent and unexpected inroads." Edna's path to full awakening is also one of sporadic and tangled growth.

Lady in black

When Edna and Adele go to the beach together they are not alone. In the distance are the lovers, a couple seen only from afar, and the lady in black, who seems to follow the lovers wherever they go. These three characters, never developed, allowed to remain as the symbols they are, appear in many of the scenes. They do not have names; they are not three-dimensional. They are symbolic of the self-absorption of lovers, and of course, of the death that follows us all. The lady in black may be the chaperone image, or even the Freudian symbol of the superego, our conscience.

Flashback to Edna's childhood

In speaking to Adele, Edna thinks of a summer day in Kentucky, of a meadow that seemed as big as the ocean. She walked through this meadow as if she was swimming. This connection of the meadow with the sea is significant. Even as a child, Edna wanted to be free of the constrictions of her life. As she talks to Adele, she loosens her collar. She is beginning to fling off the shackles of her upbringing, her sex, her private nature, her inability to confide in anyone. She can speak to Adele as she has never spoken before. These confidences are as important to Edna's awakening as the swim in the Gulf with Robert. All these events are gradually loosening Edna's habitual reserve. She tells Adele about the chilling effect of a Presbyterian service read in a spirit of gloom by her father. Obviously, her childhood lacked spontaneity. She remembers a religious period in her life and the lack of outward or spoken affectionate gestures by her family. Adele caresses her. Edna is not comfortable with the touch of her friend's hand. She is unaccustomed to loving touches. She had few friends as a child, no confidantes. She remembers an old love, a cavalry officer, another one, someone else's fiance, and a great tragedian whose picture she still has on her desk. This flashback, told us through Edna's conversation with Adele, helps us to understand why Edna has been so repressed all her life.

Marriage to Leonce Pontellier

He fell in love; she liked his loving her. She thought they had much in common; she was mistaken. Her father and sister objected to her marrying a Catholic. That was enough for Edna. She felt that this kind of marriage would take her away forever from romance and foolish dreams. We see here that Edna had a rebellious aspect even before her marriage, and that she is aware of her tendency to romance and dreams.

Narrative intrusion

"She grew fond of her husband, realizing with some unaccountable satisfaction that no trace of passion or excessive and fictitious warmth colored her affection, thereby threatening its dissolution." This observation by the narrator makes clear that Edna was always aware that passion can destroy affection, a much more lasting emotion. She married so that passion could not confuse her. This summer on Grand Isle, the dangerous emotion once again threatens to overwhelm her, and it seems as if marriage is no safeguard.

Edna's feelings toward her children

She is erratic, sometimes passionately involved with them, sometimes forgetting them completely. She doesn't usually miss them when they visit their paternal grandmother, although she experiences an occasional intense longing for them. Their absence creates in Edna a feeling of relief. She realizes her fate is to have children, although she is not suited to it at all.

Awakening theme

As Edna begins to reveal herself to Adele, the taste of candor "muddled her like wine, or like a first breath of freedom." The conversation, the intimacies, confuse and frighten her, but they are at the same time exhilarating.

Symbolism of lovers

The lovers, often in the background, completely involved with each other, are seen again. This is what it is like to be passionately in love.

CHAPTER 8

Warning theme

Adele Ratignolle tells Robert to leave Edna alone, "She is not one of us; she is not like us. She might make the unfortunate blunder of taking you seriously."

Foreshadowing

Robert is annoyed with Adele for speaking to him this way. He says he is not like Alcee Arobin. He then tells the story of Alcee and the consul's wife. Alcee is obviously a roue. Robert does not want to be put into the same category. This mention of scandalous affairs foreshadows what will happen in the novel.

Sounds

When Robert goes to his mother's room, he sees her at the sewing machine. A little black girl is sitting on the floor, working the treadle of the machine. The narrator tells us very drily that "The Creole woman does not take any chances which may be avoided of imperiling her health." This is a satiric comment on the nature of most of the women on Grand Isle. We hear the clatter of the sewing machine. This mechanical sound is the first indication of the sterility of industrialization. The other sounds we have heard have been of nature: birds, children, the sea, insects. With this new sound, which punctuates the conversation of Mme Lebrun and her son, a certain tension is set up that reflects Robert's agitation. "Bang! clatter, clatter bang!" A new and disquieting element is introduced. Victor Lebrun, Robert's younger brother, described as a "tete montee," an excitable and willful fellow, who has a temper that invites violence, is discussed. Robert offers to thrash him. We are suddenly in an atmosphere of violence with the sound of the machine in the background. A Monsieur Montel is also mentioned. He has been Madame Lebrun's suitor for twenty years and sends a message to Robert that he will be in Vera Cruz next month and that maybe Robert will join him there. The tempo of the story has changed in this chapter. There is a new quality of movement, one that has an element of danger.

CHAPTER 9

Danger of music theme

The Farival twins play the piano at a Saturday night party at which husbands, fathers, and friends are entertained. We hear the parrot's refrain again, "Get out! Get out!" Adele Ratignolle offers to play the piano so the guests can dance. She claims that she only keeps up her music so that the children will benefit. For the "mother-women," the only reason for art, or for the mastery of an instrument, is to benefit the children. With the introduction of Mademoiselle Reisz, a gifted musician, we again are offered a contrast to Edna Pontellier. Mademoiselle Reisz is a disagreeable woman, who doesn't like children and family, is quarrelsome, has poor taste in clothes, but is a very talented pianist. "Ask Mrs. Pontellier what she would like to hear me play." She seems to instinctively recognize in Edna a soul that will respond to her music. Edna, listening, is moved to tears.

In the past when Edna has heard a certain musical passage, she thought of the figure of a naked man standing beside a desolate rock. Music can stir the passions. The symbolism of the naked man, the freedom of nudity, is evoked by the sound of the music. The nudity of the man, the wildness of abandon is contrasted with the sterility of Edna's life.

When Mademoiselle Reisz plays, Edna sees no pictures of naked men. Instead "the very passions themselves were aroused within her soul, swaying it, lashing it, as the waves daily beat upon her splendid body. She trembled, she was choking, the tears blinded her." This is no polite, ladylike response. From the depths of Edna's soul comes a response that is overwhelming. When the musician asks her how she liked the music, Edna is overcome. She is unable to answer Mademoiselle Reisz. "You are the only one worth playing for. Those others. Bah!" says the irascible old woman. Edna has been loosened by the music, as she was before by the sea. Someone, perhaps Robert, then suggests that they take a bath in the ocean "at that mystic hour and under that mystic moon."

THE AWAKENING

CHAPTERS 10-22

CHAPTER 10

Gradual awakening

As Edna walks on her husband's arm to the water, she is acutely aware of Robert behind her. She realizes that she misses him when he is away from her just as "one misses the sun on a cloudy day without having thought much about the sun when it was shining." The comparison of Robert to the sun makes clear how pivotal he is becoming in Edna's life. She is gradually awakening to the fact that she is falling in love.

Music

As the summer visitors to Grand Isle enter the tepid waters of the Gulf, they can hear the faint sound of music coming from Klein's Hotel.

Odors

Strange, exotic odors assail the swimmers' senses. The sea smells, the weeds, the damp, new-plowed earth, the heavy perfume of the flowers nearby, all these combine into an aura of fecundity that is ripe with promise.

Swimming for the first time

Edna has attempted all summer to learn to swim. She was afraid of the water. But tonight she shouts for joy as she successfully swims for the first time. In fact, overwhelmed by her new power, she becomes reckless. "She wanted to swim far out, where no woman had swum before." There is no doubt about the author's intent here. Swimming, for Edna, is mastery. She can now exult in freedom, one that she has never known.

Foreshadowing

She swims out. The stretch of water frightens her, and she has a quick vision of death. She manages to return to shore.

Isolation

Changing into dry clothes, Edna leaves the rest of the guests and begins to walk away alone. She does not pay attention to the others who call to her. Robert follows her.

The spirits of the twenty-eight of August

"Did you think I was afraid?" asks Edna when Robert overtakes her. He answers that he knew she wasn't. She tells Robert how stirred she was by Mlle Reisz's playing. "I wonder if any night on earth will ever again be like this one." Robert tells her about the spirit that has haunted the Gulf, seeking a mortal for company. His search has been fruitless but Robert says that tonight this spirit found Edna. Edna is twenty-eight years old. The spirits only come out on the twenty-eighth of August. There is a kinship between these numbers. Tonight Edna has been born again. She has felt something she never experienced before. Robert and Edna sit together quietly in front of the Pontelliers' cottage. He smokes. She rocks in the hammock. It is a moment of suspended time.

CHAPTER 11

Theme of rebellion against marriage and its constraints

Leonce is surprised to find his wife still up when he returns. It is after one o'clock. She refuses to go inside with him. He comes out, orders her into the house. She refuses, stubborn and resistant. She thinks back to other times when her husband ordered her to do things, and she obeyed. This time is different. A spirit of rebellion and recklessness consumes her. She tells him never to speak to her in such a patronizing manner again. Leonce decides to join her outside, takes a glass of wine, offers some to his wife. Perhaps he is trying to make believe that all is normal. She refuses his offer. He smokes cigar after cigar. Edna begins to get tired. As her sudden blaze of stubbornness leaves her, a natural fatigue sets in. She goes in. Her husband remains.

Somehow, he has won. He has outlasted her. In this marital skirmish, his ability to wait patiently reduces Edna's gesture to a childish tantrum.

CHAPTER 12

Symbolism of lovers

Although Edna has not slept well, she is up early. Her resolve, perhaps confusing to herself, but nevertheless firm, has not vanished during the night. "She was blindly following whatever impulse moved her, as if she had placed herself in alien hands for direction, and freed her soul of responsibility." She decides to go to the Cheniere for mass. The lovers are going too. The lady in black, with her prayer book, is following them. Edna does something she has never done before. She sends for Robert. This change from her usual behavior is emphasized by the repetition in these phrases: "She had never sent for him before. She had never asked for him. She had never seemed to want him before." He joins her with "his face suffused with a quiet glow."

Theme of assertion

With this rather royal summoning of her courtier, Edna, for the first time, takes command.

Theme of journey

As they sail to the Cheniere Caminada, Edna feels as if she is being taken away from bondage. "... away from some anchorage which had held her fast, whose chains had been loosening, had snapped the night before when the mystic spirit was abroad, leaving her free to drift whithersoever she chose to set her sails."

Earthiness symbolism

Along with Edna, Robert, the lovers, the lady in black, who are all on the boat, is a young barefoot Spanish girl named Mariequita. She has a red kerchief on her head, and a basket on her arm. Robert, who knows her, talks to her in Spanish. She is described very carefully, with special attention to her bare feet, which are broad and coarse-peasant's feet. "Edna looked at her feet, and noticed the sand and slime between her brown toes." This is an earthy detail. There is something primitive about Mariequita. Edna is also experiencing some rather primitive feelings.

Foreshadowing

Mariequita asks Robert about Edna and suggests that maybe Robert and Edna are lovers. Robert hastens to assure her that Edna is married with two children. Mariequita is unimpressed with Edna's marital status. She talks about a fellow named Francisco who ran away with someone's wife, and that woman had four children. It is quite clear that to a creature such as this peasant girl, the artificial rules that men make have nothing to do with nature's rules. Edna's marriage has nothing to do with the stirrings of two animals who attract one another.

Symbolism-sails

Even the sails of the boat seem to swell. "The sails bellied taut, with the wind filling and overflowing them." Monsieur Farival, the musical twins' father, a wise old man, looks at the sails, laughs knowingly. The suggestion of full bellied sails, pregnant, is symbolic of what is beginning to happen to Edna. She is also becoming pregnant with longing.

Symbolism-animals

Robert invites Edna to go to Grand Terre the next day and look at the little wriggling gold snakes, and watch the lizards sun themselves. Snakes and lizards' are rather obvious sexual images. To use them in this way in 1899 was very daring. Today, of course, it seems rather tame.

Robert's future plans

"I'll take you some night in the pirogue [a canoe hollowed out from the trunk of a tree] when the moon shines. Maybe your Gulf spirit will whisper to you in which of these islands the treasures are hidden - direct you to the very spot, perhaps." Robert, a Creole, is full of legends, myths, fantasies such as these. He and Edna banter about what they will do with the pirate gold if they find it. Edna says she will squander it and throw it to the four winds. A recklessness is growing within her that is heady. Robert responds to her expansiveness. "We'd share it, and scatter it together," he said. His face is flushed. Mariequita, who has perhaps been intimate with both Lebrun brothers, casts a look of reproach at Robert as he laughs with Edna. Her presence makes us think of women who have been used by men, then carelessly discarded.

CHAPTER 13

Theme of oppressive religion

At the actual church service, the excuse for this outing, Edna begins to feel ill. She feels oppressed and drowsy. Her head begins to ache, and she just wants to escape the "stifling atmosphere" of the church. Robert, worried about her, suggests that she go to a Madame Antoine's where she can rest. At this stage of Edna's emergence, a church, religion, rules, orders, are not tolerable.

Theme of loosening

Madame Antoine has an immaculate tiny house. There is a huge, four-poster bed. Edna is taken to this little room, loosens her clothes, and takes off most of them. She bathes her face, neck, and arms in the basin, and takes off her shoes and stockings, climbing into the very center of the high white bed. She looks at her own round arms, and sees the texture of the skin, almost as if she is seeing them for the first time. And, of course, she is. This is the first time she has looked at her own body with a keen sense of sensuality. She falls asleep, aware always of Robert's presence nearby. Her body, sinking into deep sleep, is utterly relaxed, almost as if drugged. She sleeps for a long time, refreshes herself with powder, looks in the mirror, and sees a glowing face. She is very hungry, and eats a crusty brown loaf and a bottle of wine. The description of her eating is detailed and sensual. There is a suggestion here of the symbolism of the Christian mass. Edna's appetite for food, for life, is growing. She senses a change in herself. "How many years have I slept?" she asks Robert.

Robert as protector

Robert tells Edna that he has been guarding her slumbers. The rest of the party they came with has all left to return to Grand Isle. Edna idly wonders whether her husband will worry about her whereabouts. Robert assures her he will not. They do not rush to return. Madame Antoine tells them wonderful Creole stories. When Edna and Robert leave, it is dark. "... misty spirit forms were prowling in the shadows and among the reeds, and upon the water were phantom ships, speeding to cover." The entire day has had a magical quality. Not once has Edna thought about her children.

CHAPTER 14

Leonce's indifference

At first when Edna does not return from Cheniere Caminada with the others, Leonce is "uneasy," but he is easily dissuaded from going to the island himself to look for his wife and occupies himself at Klein's, discussing "securities, exchanges, stocks, bonds, or something of the sort." Adele Ratignolle dismisses his masculine concerns, which also reduces his activities to negligible occupations. Certainly he doesn't seem unduly worried or disturbed by his wife's absence.

Theme of awakening

Edna says good night to Robert and asks him an important question: "Do you know we have been together the whole livelong day, Robert - since early this morning?" She seems to be clarifying for herself and for Robert how special their relationship has become. She realizes that in some way she is different, is seeing things in a new way. The song she hums to herself is "Ah! Si tu savais!" and that is precisely what is happening. She is beginning to know herself.

CHAPTER 15
Revelation

Robert decides, rather precipitously, to leave Grand Isle for Mexico. Although he has spent the day with Edna, he has not mentioned anything about his plans to her. She is dismayed and puzzled by his abrupt departure. When he comes to her cottage to say goodbye, he seems ill at ease, and eager to be off, afraid of an involvement with Edna. She recognizes her own infatuation, understands that she had feelings like this in the past, but is unable to control her growing passion for this young man.

CHAPTER 16
Rebellion theme

After Robert leaves, Edna comforts herself by swimming. This activity provides her with the only pleasurable diversion she has now that Robert is gone. The meaning, the color have gone out of her life. She talks about Robert rather shamelessly, to everyone, going to Madame Lebrun's room and looking at his baby pictures. A letter sent to his mother fascinates her although he has not sent any special greeting to Edna. She confides to Adele that, "I would give up the unessential; I would give my money, I would give my life for my children; but I wouldn't give myself. I can't make it more clear; it's only something which I am beginning to comprehend, which is revealing itself to me." This statement shows that Edna will fight for her independence and for freedom from the constraints of motherhood. She will not submerge her new-found self in anyone.

Foil character-Mademoiselle Reisz

Chopin uses character foils skillfully. Both Mademoiselle Reisz, the independent woman, a talented musician, unmarried and unbeholden to any man, and Adele Ratignolle, the "mother-woman," are used for deliberate contrasts to Edna. She is like neither one of these foils and cannot become like them, even if she wished. Mademoiselle Reisz is a somewhat unpleasant woman, who won't swim, complains about the food, but becomes interested in Edna and invites her to visit when they return to New Orleans.

CHAPTER 17

Contrast in setting

The scene shifts here to the Pontelliers' home in New Orleans, which is luxurious, meticulously tended, and utterly conventional. Here there will be restraints on Edna.

Leonce's acquisitiveness

Edna's husband enjoys his home and its appointments. He is careful to maintain it, and is described as valuing his possessions, not so much for their intrinsic beauty, but because they are his. In much the same way, he values his wife.

| Rebellion

On Tuesday afternoons, Edna is supposed to be "at home," which means that callers come, women who bring their calling cards, drink a liqueur or coffee, and chat. For six years Edna has been a gracious hostess. A few weeks after returning to New Orleans, Edna abruptly stops receiving guests on Tuesdays. She offers no excuse, either to her guests, or to Leonce, who is astonished at her behavior. Leonce tells Edna that he cannot afford to offend the people who come to call; he does business with them. She is unimpressed. She has defied her husband and **convention**. When Leonce complains about the food the cook has prepared, Edna does not try to placate her husband as she once would have done. Instead she eats alone, goes to her room, takes off her wedding ring, flings it upon the carpet, stamps her heel on it, but she is unable to make a mark on the "little glittering circlet." She breaks a glass vase. She wants to destroy something. When the maid finds the ring and gives it to Edna, she puts it back on. She is not yet ready to escape from her marriage.

CHAPTER 18

| Households contrasted

Edna goes to visit Adele Ratignolle at her home in New Orleans. She intends to maintain the friendship with Adele that blossomed on Grand Isle. The Ratignolles are very compatible, even finishing sentences for each other. "The Ratignolles understood each other perfectly. If ever the fusion of two human beings into one has been accomplished on this sphere it was surely in their union." This glimpse into another marriage depresses Edna. The domestic harmony she sees does not fill her with longing. She finds it horribly boring, and actually is filled with sympathy for her friend who lives a "colorless existence which never uplifted its possessor beyond the region of blind contentment, in which no moment of anguish ever visited her soul, in which she would never have the taste of life's delirium." Edna does not want this kind of life. She wants more.

CHAPTER 19

Leonce's reaction to Edna's art

Edna spends her time in her atelier [studio] working on her sketches. She makes no attempt to run her household in the manner she had before. Her refusal to entertain and her disinterest in returning the visits of those who call upon her anger her husband, but she refuses to accommodate his wishes. He cannot understand why she should want to spend all her time painting, when she should be taking care of her family. "I feel like painting," answered Edna. "Perhaps I shan't always feel like it." He continues to remonstrate with her. He cannot understand why she can't paint the way Adele Ratignolle "keeps up her music." Her friend doesn't let the household deteriorate, and Leonce hastens to assure Edna that Adele is far more of a musician than she will ever be a painter.

Edna's understanding of her art

Edna does not try to defend her painting. She understands it for what it is. Leonce begins to wonder if his wife isn't becoming mentally unbalanced, but he does leave her alone. Edna spends days working in her atelier, and disrupts the entire household, demanding they all pose for her, but she is completely dissatisfied with her work. She is haunted by memories of Grand Isle, and by physical desire. In spite of this, there are days when she is very happy just to be alive. She responds to the sun, the warmth, the beauty of the city, and wanders alone exploring places that are strange and unfamiliar. She frequently sings the **refrain**, "Ah! si tu savais!" She is beginning to know.

CHAPTER 20

Robert's younger brother

Edna decides to visit Mademoiselle Reisz. She wants to hear her play again. Unfortunately, she has lost her address. It occurs to her that Mademoiselle Lebrun might have it, and since this gives her a perfect opportunity to visit the Lebruns in New Orleans, she goes to their home. The house is described as looking like a prison, with iron bars before the door and lower windows. If it is not a prison, it is a place that is tightly guarding something that Edna wants. Victor, Robert's nineteen-year-old brother, greets Edna warmly and entertains her with slightly risque stories of his romantic escapades. He attempts to draw Edna into his confidence by winking at her while she is speaking to his mother. The Lebruns tell Edna about two letters they have received from Robert in Mexico, but there is no mention of Edna in either one of them, and she begins to feel despondent. Victor seems to be an exaggeration of Robert-flirtatious, reckless, impetuous. Both sons have an aura about them of provocative sensuality. Victor also seems able to sense in Edna that she will listen to his tales of conquests. He titillates her the way Robert did on Grand Isle. He is a reminder of his older brother.

CHAPTER 21

Symbolism of Mademoiselle Reisz's apartment

Mademoiselle Reisz, an independent woman of great musical talent, lives in an apartment on the top floor. The rooms have plenty of windows, even though they are dingy. A great deal of light and air comes through them, and from the windows can be seen "the crescent of the river, the masts of ships and the big chimneys of the Mississippi steamers." There is a view here, unknown in other more conventional rooms. Here, there is freedom and the opportunity to see things that others do not. The apartment is symbolic of another way of life, less stifling. A magnificent grand piano crowds the apartment, asserting the importance of music to Mademoiselle Reisz.

The courageous soul

Mademoiselle Reisz banters amiably with Edna. When Edna reveals that she has been painting, Mademoiselle Reisz is scornful of her pretensions. An artist, she says, must have a courageous soul, must be willing to defy **convention**. She does not feel that Edna has this quality.

Love letter

Robert Lebrun has written to Mademoiselle Reisz. His letter is full of questions about Edna. He also asks Mademoiselle Reisz to play Chopin's "Impromptu" for her as this is music that has stirred him. Although he never says he is in love with Edna, this letter, full of Edna's name, is obviously a letter from a man who simply must write his beloved's name again and again. After much coaxing, Mademoiselle Reisz lets Edna see the letter. She plays the "Impromptu" while Edna reads the letter, and the combination of the music and of Robert's words reduces Edna to tears. Mademoiselle Reisz seems aware of Edna's infatuation and does not discourage her at all. She invites her to come back whenever she feels like it.

CHAPTER 22

Theme: men cannot understand women

Leonce seeks help from Doctor Mandelet, an old friend and the family physician. He complains about Edna and her attitude. "She's got some sort of notion in her head concerning the eternal rights of women; and - you understand -we meet in the morning at the breakfast table." With this admission, Leonce reveals his inability to understand his wife, and he discloses that Edna is no longer sleeping with him. Leonce also complains that Edna refuses to attend her sister's wedding, saying that a wedding "is one of the most lamentable spectacles on earth." Dr. Mandelet suggests that maybe Edna is associating with pseudo-intellectual women who are filling her head with foolish ideas. When Leonce assures him that this is not the case, that actually, Edna has stopped socializing, and does not want to associate with anyone, the doctor becomes worried. He suggests maybe there is something genetically wrong. Leonce says he chose her carefully; she comes of good sound stock. This remark clearly shows Leonce's acquisitiveness. Before he married, he checked his wife's lineage, almost as if he were checking that a horse he was purchasing would be a good breeder. The doctor sympathizes with Leonce and they agree that women are very strange. They are "moody and whimsical," and cannot be understood. He advises Leonce to take Edna with him on a business trip, if she wishes to go, or to let her stay home, if she doesn't want to accompany him.

    The doctor suspects there may be another man involved, but would never suggest this possibility to a Creole husband. This chapter shows how impossible it is for either of these men to understand what Edna is and what she is going through.

THE AWAKENING

CHAPTERS 23–31

CHAPTER 23

Edna's relationship with her father

When Edna's father comes to visit, Edna spends a great deal of time with him, not because she is so fond of him, but because they have certain tastes in common, one of them being horse racing. The father, once a colonel in the Confederate Army, still retains a military bearing, but his clothing is padded, which "gave a fictitious breadth to his shoulders and chest." His clothes make him appear to be more than he really is. He is not a substantial man, not a caring or sensitive father, and he had not been a loving husband. He agrees to pose for Edna in her atelier, but expects his daughter to be talented, simply because she is his daughter. His possessiveness seems similar to Leonce's feelings about Edna. Neither man recognizes her for what she is, but merely as an ornamental addition to himself. He does not seem particularly interested in his grandchildren either.

Flirtation

When Edna takes her father to the Ratignolles for a musical evening, Adele flirts with the Colonel until "the Colonel's old head felt thirty years younger on his padded shoulders." Edna does not understand this at all. She is not a flirt and does not have any of these feminine wiles.

Animal symbolism

Doctor Mandelet is invited to the Pontellier's home to meet the Colonel. He notices a change in Edna. She is no longer the listless person he knew. She has been transformed into a radiant woman, pulsing with the forces of life. "She reminded him of some beautiful, sleek animal waking up in the sun." Edna is awakening, and it is becoming obvious to the doctor, trained as he is to be sensitive to such things. The animalism in the description of Edna, the hint of muscles rippling, of power and force, hidden, but emerging, is highly suggestive and provocative.

Stories

The guests amuse themselves at the dinner table by telling stories. The Colonel relates stories of his escapades in the war. He, of course, always plays a very prominent part. The doctor tells of a woman, looking for new outlets, who returns to her old love. The narrator observes in this that this particular story didn't impress Edna. Edna tells a story of a woman who paddles away with her lover one night in a pirogue and never comes back. As she relates it, the people listening can actually feel the sensuous details of the southern night, the movement of the pirogue through the water, the bird's wings, the faces of the lovers. Edna's story is striking in its **imagery** and, of course, in its **theme** of lovers escaping. The doctor is sorry that he accepted the invitation. "He did not want the secrets of other lives thrust upon him." He feels sure that Edna has a lover. "I hope it isn't Arobin," he mutters to himself.

CHAPTER 24

Refusal to attend wedding

Edna's father and husband are horrified at her refusal to attend her sister's wedding. She offers no excuse, and when the Colonel leaves for the wedding, Edna is glad. Leonce leaves shortly to be at the wedding and to atone for Edna's action. The two men have talked about Edna's behavior and the father-in-law tells Leonce that he is far too lenient. "Authority, coercion are what is needed. Put your foot down good and hard; the only way to manage a wife. Take my word for it." Leonce feels that the Colonel may have coerced his wife into her grave. He is certainly not as insensitive a man as his father-in-law.

Edna's ambivalence

Before Leonce's departure, Edna grows very affectionate and concerned about his welfare. In fact, she busies herself with his packing and clothes and underwear, quite as "Madame Ratignolle would have done under similar circumstances." She cries when he leaves, and suspects that she may join him in New York where he is going after her sister's wedding. She manifests a lot of ambivalence in her feelings toward her husband, remembering his many acts of kindness and affection.

Relief

The children have been taken away by the paternal grandmother and so Edna is alone. "A feeling that was unfamiliar but very delicious came over her." She explores her own home, works in the garden, plays with the dog, spends time in the kitchen with the cook and dines alone. She enjoys her dinner enormously. Although she thinks about Leonce and the children, she is content to be alone, and seems to relish her solitude. She makes up her mind to read more. She has a feeling of peace she has never had before.

CHAPTER 25

Alcee Arobin

Edna goes to the races with Alcee Arobin, a young man of fashion. He spends his time at the race track, the opera, the fashionable clubs. He has a somewhat insolent manner, a good figure, is not "overburdened with depth of thought or feeling." (The narrator's offhanded comment is, as always, a welcome intrusion). He had seen Edna before and found her unapproachable, but after meeting her at the races, recently, with her father, he decided to call on her and ask her to go to the races with him. Although they have Mrs. Highcamp with them (the author is obviously having some fun with the name), this lady is being used by Alcee Arobin to cover him with some respectability.

Edna's excitement

The races excite Edna. She is quite knowledgeable about horses, having being brought up in Kentucky horse country, and she plays for very high stakes and wins that day. She becomes feverish from excitement, and people turn to look at her, hoping for a "tip." Alcee catches Edna's excitement. They have dinner together and Alcee takes her home. He makes plans to go to the races again with Edna.

Appetite

Edna is hungry after this evening with Alcee. Although she has eaten dinner at the Highcamps, it wasn't enough. She eats cheese and crackers, drinks beer. She is extremely restless and excited. All her senses seem to be clamoring for satisfaction. She is unable to sleep well. Her appetites are sharpening.

First contact with Alcee

When Alcee calls again, they go to the races alone, without Mrs. Highcamp. Alcee returns home with Edna, and he begins to woo her. He shows her an old saber scar he received in a duel outside of Paris. Obviously he is trying to impress her with his romantic, reckless past. She touches the scar, touching his palm. She is very agitated after this, and yet Alcee recognizes in her face something that does not discourage his advances. She tells him that she doesn't like him and wants him to go. Then she apologizes, saying that something in her manner must have misled him in some way. He replies that she hasn't misled him. His own emotions have done that. The narrator comments wryly that "Alcee Arobin's manner was so genuine that it often deceived even himself."

Memories of Robert

Edna feels she has somehow betrayed Robert. She does not think about her husband. It is not the same thing because she never loved her husband.

Sensual response

Although she is upset about Alcee's presumption, she cannot forget his presence, his manners, the warmth of his glances, and above all the touch of his lips upon her hand, which has acted as a narootic upon her. She sleeps a languorous sleep.

Language

The language in this chapter is filled with words that evoke sensuality. Words such as "fever," "flamed," "intoxicant," "restless," "excited," "sensuousness," "narcotic," "languorous" all contribute to the heightened feelings Edna is experiencing.

CHAPTER 26

Passion

Alcee's attentions continue. Edna allows him to speak to her in a way that shocks her at first, but "in a way that pleased her at last, appealing to the animalism that stirred impatiently within her."

Edna's "Room Of Her Own"

Edna visits Mademoiselle Reisz in an effort to quiet her inner turmoil. The musician seems fond of her and is completely aware of Edna's infatuation. One cold miserable afternoon, she announces her intention to move away from her house. Mademoiselle Reisz questions her as to where she is going, and Edna tells her that there is a little four-room house right around the corner from her husband's house. Mademoiselle Reisz wants to know why she is doing this, and Edna says that her husband's house is not hers. Because she has a little money of her own, has won money at the races, and has started to sell some of her sketches, she can afford her own place. She plans to move there with one old servant. Above all, she wants the feeling of freedom and independence. She has not told her husband.

Last grand dinner

Edna plans to give a dinner at which all of her friends shall eat, drink, sing, and laugh. This dinner will be significant for them all. It will be held at her husband's house.

Robert's letters

Edna reads the letters that Robert continues to send to Mademoiselle Reisz. He does not write directly to Edna. She learns that he is returning to New Orleans. She is delighted and confesses her infatuation to Mademoiselle Reisz, who points out what an ordinary young man Robert is. Edna defends him and her love. She says that women do not choose whom they fall in love with.

Edna's family

Edna sends candy to her children. She writes a tender message on a card. It appears to be the first time she has remembered them. She also writes to her husband, revealing her plans to leave, "for a while," and regretting that he will not be available to help her with the farewell dinner. She seems remarkably self-involved, and unaware of the effect her decision will have on her family. The narrator's comment on how cheerful and brilliant the letter is clearly reveals Edna's total immersion in herself.

CHAPTER 27

Consummation

Edna permits Alcee to take more liberties with her person. He touches her hair, her cheeks, her chin. She permits it while wondering about herself. She questions whether she is wicked. She says she cannot convince herself that she is. Mademoiselle Reisz has told her, she confides in Alcee, that in order to soar above the level plain of tradition and prejudice one must have strong wings. Mademoiselle Reisz does not think that Edna has these wings. Alcee continues to fondle Edna. They kiss. "It was the first kiss of her life to which her nature had really responded. It was a flaming torch that kindled desire."

CHAPTER 28

The shortest chapter

Less than one page, this chapter describes Edna's feelings after that passionate kiss. Chopin is discreet about what might have happened. After all, the author was writing in 1899. As daring as Chopin is, she would not describe graphically the details of a physical relationship. It is left to the reader's imagination. We are told that Edna cries after Alcee leaves her; she has an immense sense of irresponsibility; she feels that the unexpected and shocking have occurred. Although she thinks of her husband, she is consumed by an even fiercer love for Robert. But above all, she understands herself. She sees that life is made up of beauty and brutality. She feels neither shame nor remorse. There is regret because "it was not the kiss of love which had inflamed her, because it was not love which had held this cup of life to her lips." Certainly, this kind of reaction indicates that more than a kiss took place, even though the author continues to be guarded about the details of what happened. Edna knows herself for the first time. She knows she is capable of animal passion, completely devoid of love.

CHAPTER 29

Independence

Without waiting to hear from her husband and learn how he will react to her decision to quit his house, Edna hurriedly packs her things in preparation for her move to her new home. She feels uncomfortable in this house. She no longer belongs here. She must leave. She takes only her own things, not anything of her husband's.

Alcee's attempt to help

When Alcee visits her that afternoon (he does not seem to have to earn a living), he finds Edna absorbed in her packing. He offers to help her, and a scene follows in which he puts on a dust cap, mounts a ladder, takes down pictures and curtains, while Edna laughs at him. She seems very much in control of the situation, does not allow him to assume command. He refers to the upcoming farewell dinner as a "coup d'etat." Edna plans to let Leonce pay the bills. She allows Alcee to continue to hope for a continuation of their affair. Alcee seems puzzled at her manner. He expected her to be reproachful, or tearful. Instead she is utterly in command, ordering him around. There seems to be a complete reversal of roles. Far from being wracked with guilt at what has occurred, Edna seems independent and sure of herself.

CHAPTER 30

The guests

Edna's dinner is a small affair: ten guests. Adele is advanced in her pregnancy and cannot attend and Mademoiselle Lebrun sends her regrets at the last minute. Alcee, Mrs. Highcamp, Mademoiselle Reisz, Monsieur Ratignolle, Victor Lebrun, a Mr. and Mrs. Merriman, characters we have not met before, along with a Miss Mayblunt, an intellectual, and a gentleman who is a journalist, are the guests. It is a rather odd assortment.

Bacchanalian setting

The table is gorgeous with a splendid pale yellow satin lace cloth, and massive candles, under yellow silk shades. Full roses glow yellow and gold, and silver and gold silverware and crystal glasses sparkle. The ordinary stiff dining-chairs have been replaced by soft luxurious ones. There is the feeling of a bacchanalian feast, of sensuous beauty, of lavishness, about the setting.

Edna's appearance

Edna is wearing a magnificent cluster of diamonds in her hair. She admits that it is a gift from her husband that has just arrived this morning. She is twenty-nine today. Edna is wearing a golden satin gown. Her skin has a glow of vibrancy. She looks regal.

Music

Edna has hired musicians to play during the dinner. They are not in the room, but they provide an agreeable accompaniment to the conversation and to the meal. The soft splash of a fountain is heard also. A heavy odor of Jessamine (jasmine) comes through the open windows. The author's use of sensory details creates a scene that is voluptuous and stimulating.

Depression

Amidst this opulence, Edna feels a hopelessness overtaking her. It is a familiar feeling. She is filled with an acute longing to see Robert.

Childbirth

Monsieur Ratignolle has to leave early, saying his wife is momentarily expecting their child. He mentions that she has a "vague dread" which only his presence can dispel. This interjection of the physical consequences of sex for women seems to break the spell of the evening. It is a return to the mundane, away from the exotic.

Victor's appearance

Mrs. Highcamp places a garland of roses, yellow and red, on Victor's black curls. It transforms him into a vision of exotic beauty. His cheeks, his eyes glow with a fire. When a white silken scarf is placed on him, he appears to be a "graven image of desire." He drinks wine, agrees to sing a song to the assembled company, and begins to sing, "Ah! Si tu savais!" Edna is very disturbed by the **refrain**, puts her glass down so abruptly that it shatters, but Victor continues to sing. She goes over to him, puts her hand over his mouth. He kisses her palm. The guests leave. This party has had overtones of Oriental sumptuousness, a lavish display of sensuality, and a pagan delight in the senses.

CHAPTER 31

Sexual symbolism

When the guests leave, Edna and Alcee straighten up the room after the party. It is a domestic scene, but Edna is disheartened and doesn't speak. She feels depressed but is much aware of Alcee's physical presence. As they walk over together to the pigeon house, she notices the "black line of his leg moving in and out so close to her against the yellow shimmer of her gown." This sexual symbolism reveals the true nature of their relationship. But there is another symbol here too. Alcee has invaded her territory. He is encroaching on her person.

The pigeon house

The little house that Edna has moved to is a simple place, far removed from the splendor of her husband's home. Edna has made it comfortable and habitable, but it is not luxurious. When Edna and Alcee enter this evening, Edna is surprised to find that it is filled with flowers that Alcee has sent her. She does not seem particularly pleased at this further invasion of Alcee into her space. She seems tired and says she is miserable. Alcee sympathizes with her and says that he will leave her, but he begins to caress her, and she allows him to remain. "He did not say good night until she had become supple to his gentle, seductive entreaties." Chopin's use of sibilants in this sentence (the repeated use of s) creates a mood of snake-like seduction.

THE AWAKENING

CHAPTERS 32-38

CHAPTER 32

Leonce's response to Edna's departure

Leonce writes his wife a letter of disapproval. He is much concerned with what people will say. He warns her that a scandal might do damage to his business prospects. Feeling that Edna has been acting strangely, and that he must protect his reputation, he decides to hire an architect to remodel his home, and puts a notice in the papers that due to the inconvenience of having workmen in their home, the Pontelliers will be leaving New Orleans for the summer. He has managed to save face, and at the same time have some work done on his home, which he had wanted to do for a long time. Obviously, Leonce is a resourceful man, and his concern for appearances has been satisfied.

Edna's feelings about her new home

Edna feels happy in her modest home. "There was with her a feeling of having descended in the social scale, with a corresponding sense of having risen in the spiritual." The casting off of obligations and the indifference to other people's opinions have freed her.

Visit to children

This is the only place in the book where Edna seems to have strong maternal feelings. She enjoys the feel of her children, and cannot look at her two little sons enough. Her eyes are hungry. She listens to their tales, and goes with them to see the pigs and cows; she spends a week with the children, and it seems to be the best week she has ever had with them. She tells about the house and how it is filled with workmen, and assures them about their precious possessions. They want to know about the house she is living in. Edna's mother-in-law is delighted that her grandchildren will remain with her until the renovations on the house are completed. It is difficult for Edna to part with the boys, and on the trip home, she hears their voices, and feels their cheeks. But when she returns to the pigeon house, she is alone and the children's voices have faded. At the end of this chapter, she seems, once again, to have removed herself from the children.

CHAPTER 33

Adele's warning

Although she is rapidly approaching the end of her pregnancy, Adele comes to see Edna in the pigeon house. She is very curious and confused about Edna's motives for the move. She says that Edna, in many ways, is like a child, and doesn't reflect enough upon her actions. She also warns her about living alone, and allowing Alcee to spend so much time with her. She again mentions his reputation as a womanizer, but Edna does not seem concerned. Adele begs Edna to come to her when she goes into labor, and Edna agrees to, no matter what time of day or night it is.

Robert's return

At Mademoiselle Reisz' apartment, one afternoon, while Edna is waiting for the musician to return, the door opens and Robert enters. He has returned from Mexico, and Edna is shocked to learn that he has been back for two days. He has not contacted her, and Edna doesn't understand why. She thought he would want to see her immediately. Robert appears to be uncomfortable, and does not act in the same manner that he had during the summer on Grand Isle. When she asks him why he didn't write to her, he says that he cannot imagine that his letters would be of any interest to her. They leave together and Edna invites Robert to have dinner with her in the pigeon house. He seems reluctant to do so, but finally agrees. When he notices a photograph of Alcee in the house, he seems shocked. Edna says that she is sketching him, and is using the photograph. She discovers that Robert was disappointed in his business ventures in Mexico, and that is why he has returned. She had hoped he returned because of her. She begins to bait him, repeating some of his own words to him, and they fall into an uncomfortable silence as they wait for dinner.

CHAPTER 34

Jealousy

In the pigeon house, a "certain degree of ceremony settled upon them with the announcement of dinner." There is constraint and tension between Edna and Robert due to his deliberate holding back. Edna is far more forthright about her feelings. She is confused and angered by Robert's aloofness. The only thing he admits is that he has forgotten nothing of Grand Isle. Edna notices that he is using an intricately designed tobacco pouch, and intuits that it has been given to him by a woman. She questions him about the extent of his involvement. Robert doesn't deny the pouch was a gift from a woman, but he says it was not important. Edna is filled with jealousy.

Alcee meets Robert

Alcee Arobin drops in with a message from Mrs. Merriman who has had to postpone a card party. He exhibits a degree of familiarity with Edna that Robert finds disturbing. A tension-filled discussion about women ensues between the two men, and Edna taunts them both about their romantic escapades. Robert gets up rather quickly to leave but he mentions Mr. Pontellier before he goes, in what sounds like a deliberate reminder to both Edna and Alcee of Edna's married state. Edna and Alcee enact a little domestic scene in which he reads items to her from the newspaper, while she straightens up the table. He again tells her how he adores her. She ignores him. His protestations of love are always amusingly cynical. When she says that he must have told the same things to many women, he says "I have said it before, but I don't think I ever came so near meaning it." When he leaves, Edna is consumed with jealousy about Robert's liaisons in Mexico. She is bitterly disappointed in their reunion.

CHAPTER 35

Symbolism of clothing

When Edna awakes the next morning, she has shaken off her mood of jealousy and despondency. She convinces herself that Robert still loves her, and is confident that she will be able to break through his reserve. She knows that her passion for him will make him admit his own. Half-dressed, she eats breakfast. It is instructive to note Chopin's use of clothing. When Edna is feeling a sense of freedom, she casts off her clothing. We have seen this in other scenes: her first confidences to Adele, her visit to Cheniere Caminada.

Birth symbolism

Edna receives three letters that morning, one from her son Raoul, who tells her about the birth of ten tiny white pigs, and who asks his mother to send him candy. Birth symbolism is used frequently by Chopin. Edna is being reborn throughout the book. Adele is about to give birth; the sow gives birth. A feeling of fecundity adds to the sensuosity of the novel.

Letters

Edna enjoys her son's letters. She also receives one from her husband, in which he makes plans for a trip to Europe. He assures her that this trip will be a luxurious one. He will not have to economize since he has done well in the stock market. Obviously he is trying to distract his wife with the promise of a longed-for trip. Leonce uses whatever means he can to try and lure Edna back to his home. Money is what Leonce has, and he doesn't hesitate to use it to protect his marriage.

Edna answers him evasively. Arobin also writes to her. She makes no reply, but burns it. She doesn't care about him.

Robert's indifference

Robert does not come to see her. She waits patiently for him, determined not to seek him out herself. She does continue to see Alcee Arobin.

Alcee's horses

Although she is indifferent to Alcee, she sees him when he calls. She goes out driving with him. His horses are a little unmanageable. She finds the drive exciting. They return home early and Chopin comments that "it was late when he left her." What happened in the interim is left to the reader's imagination, but the narrator mentions that Arobin is intrigued with Edna: "... he detected the latent sensuality, which unfolded under his delicate sense of her nature's requirements like a torpid, torrid, sensitive blossom." This kind of narrative comment was heady stuff in 1899.

CHAPTER 36

Garden symbolism

There is a little garden in the suburbs where Edna goes to dream, to read, to think of Robert. Few people know about it. Edna has discovered it on one of her solitary walks. Few women at that time walked by themselves. Edna is unique in this small act of independence. The garden is sheltered, quiet, idyllic. It is symbolic of an innocent place where Edna can go to dream of her love.

Fate

Robert enters the garden one day, completely unexpectedly. He says he too often comes to this garden. It is fate that has brought them together again. Neither of them had planned to meet here. Edna, taken by surprise, confronts Robert and asks him why he doesn't come to see her, why he has neglected her so badly since his return from Mexico. He seems angry and asks her why she is so intent on forcing a confession from him that can result in nothing. He says she is asking him to bare a wound. Edna now realizes that he does indeed love her, and she stops questioning him.

Confession

They return to Edna's home. Edna kisses Robert tenderly. He cannot help responding to her embrace. He says that he has kept away because she is married, and what good can it do to admit his love. He mentions marriage to her, if Leonce would only set her free. Edna is astonished. She tells Robert that Leonce cannot set her free. She is not one of his possessions. She is already free. "I give myself where I choose." It seems that it was never Edna's intention to marry Robert; she wants to love him. Robert is more conventional.

Breakdown

A message arrives at that moment from Adele. She has gone into labor, and wants Edna to come to her. Edna, having promised her friend, leaves Robert, who begs her to stay. He has completely broken down at this point, and wants nothing more than to caress and hold Edna. She seems much stronger than he and will not break her promise to Adele. It is interesting to note that her marriage vows to Leonce do not concern her at all.

CHAPTER 37

Symbolism of childbirth

Edna finds Adele in great distress, complaining bitterly about being neglected. She has a nurse, her husband, and the doctor, but she still feels abandoned. She is restless, and berates everyone who is trying to help her. Edna begins to feel uncomfortable, thinking of her own labors, the pain, the odor of chloroform, the birth of a new life, "added to the great unnumbered multitude of souls that come and go." This childbirth scene makes her remember her own role as a mother, and it is one she prefers not to think about at this time. She feels an immense revolt against the ways of Nature, realizing how a woman who is a mother can never free herself from her responsibilities. Edna has recently given birth to herself, as she came to understand her own nature, and this birth, for her, is the most important one, not the birth of a baby.

Adele's reminder

When Adele gives birth, she whispers to Edna, "Think of the children, Edna. Oh think of the children! Remember them." Adele obviously senses that Edna is about to do something reckless, and in spite of her own exhaustion following the birth, warns Edna.

CHAPTER 38

Edna's confusion

Edna walks home after the birth with Doctor Mandelet. He says that Adele should never have demanded that Edna witness the birth. It was cruel to ask that of her friend. Edna replies that one must think of the children. The scene she has just witnessed has made her think of her own children, and of the obligation she has to them. It is not a thought she wishes to entertain. The doctor reminds Edna how Nature's only concern is to procure mothers for the race. This conversation clarifies for Edna how transitory passion can be, and how permanent the products of passion are. When Doctor Mandelet offers her help, she says that she doesn't want to speak of things that are troubling her. She expresses her thanks for his help, but says that she wants things her own way. That is asking for a great deal, she knows, but "I shouldn't want to trample upon the little lives. Oh! I don't know what I'm saying, Doctor. Good night. Don't blame me for anything."

Robert's letter

Edna returns to her house and thinks again of Robert and their last passionate embraces. She once again thinks that nothing on earth could be better than "possession of the loved one." She hopes that he is waiting for her. She plans to awaken him with kisses. He is not there. Instead he has left her a brief letter. "I love you. Good-bye-because I love you." Edna does not sleep at all that night. The reader is not told what she is thinking about. We do not know at this point what she will do. The only commentary from the narrator is a description of her sleepless night, and the fact that she is still awake in the morning when her maid comes to light the fire.

CHAPTER 39

Return to Grand Isle

The last chapter of *The Awakening* returns the reader to the setting of the first chapter. Once again we are on Grand Isle. Victor Lebrun, Robert's brother, is repairing some of the cottages on the resort island in preparation for the summer season. He and Mariequita are talking about the dinner at Mrs. Pontellier's. Victor is exaggerating every detail, and Mariequita becomes quite jealous. She feels envious of Mrs. Pontellier's beauty and easy conquest of men. The two young people are astonished when Edna Pontellier suddenly appears. They have just been talking about her. And here she is. But this is no entrancing spectacle. Edna looks tired and worn out. She tells them that she has come for a few days to rest. Before dinner, she says, she wants to take a swim. They tell her that the water is too cold, but she says she will just put her toes in.

Narrative comment

The reader is now told what Edna thought about during that last sleepless night. She realized that her nature meant she would want many lovers. Although she was not concerned about Leonce and the harm this would do to him, she was concerned about her sons. Since she cannot reconcile her passionate nature with that of a mother, she becomes despondent. She even realizes that her passion for Robert will one day pass. Her children seem like antagonists who will overcome, who will enslave her. She decides to elude them.

Symbolism of nudity

Edna walks down to the beach and removes her bathing suit. It is the first time she has ever been naked in the open air. She feels like a newborn person. Edna is about to become completely free for the first time in her life. It is fitting that she strips herself of the encumbrance of clothing.

Whitmanesque passage

As she steps into the ocean, she feels the sensuousness of the water, which enfolds her in a "soft, close embrace." The sea is described as "seductive, never ceasing, whispering, clamoring, murmuring, inviting the soul to wander in abysses of solitude." This passage is very similar to parts of Whitman's "Song of Myself." It is known that Chopin was an admirer of Whitman, and was familiar with his work.

Freedom

Edna swims out too far. She swims with long sweeping strokes. She is not afraid, except for one moment of terror, which passes. She does not look back but she thinks of Leonce and the children. They will not possess her. Her last thoughts are of her childhood, her father, her sister, the barking of a dog. She hears the hum of bees and smells the "musky odor of pinks." Her death is a deliberate, conscious decision. There is no quality of hysteria here, but a sense of dignity and peace that bring a measure of grandeur to Edna. Unable to go back to a life as a conventional wife and mother, Edna chooses freedom in death. It is her choice.

THE AWAKENING

CHARACTER ANALYSIS

EDNA PONTELLIER

A handsome, rather than conventionally pretty, twenty-eight-year-old woman, Edna Pontellier is vacationing on the island of Grand Isle, a resort for wealthy Creole families off the coast of Louisiana with her husband and two young sons. She is not Creole; she was born in Kentucky into a Presbyterian family. Edna's mother died when she was quite young; her father was a stern man, who ruled the household in an oppressive manner. Deprived of her mother's love at an early age, she was brought up in an atmosphere of gloom that had a chilling effect on her development as a woman. Although she had three infatuations before her marriage, none of them was ever acknowledged. She grew up without love of passion and her marriage to Leonce Pontellier is as repressive as her childhood had been. She was not in love with her husband when she married him. Nor is she in love with him now. She amuses herself flirting with Robert Lebrun, the son of the resort owner. Married women in this Creole society often play this game - it is not taken seriously by anyone. Edna is mildly titillated by Robert's attention, and she gradually begins to awaken to her own sexuality. She learns to swim during this summer, is stirred deeply by music, begins to paint more seriously than she has ever done before, and finally convinces herself that she is madly in love with Robert. She allows herself to be seduced by Alcee Arobin, a well-known roue, when Robert becomes frightened by her passion. Understanding her sensual nature, and finally facing her own sexual hunger, Edna, unable to reconcile her appetites with her role as wife and mother, swims out to sea and drowns. It is deliberately done; her death is not an accident.

LEONCE PONTELLIER

Forty years old, a successful broker in New Orleans, Leonce is proud of his wife's beauty and considers her a possession. He expects her to be a conventional wife and to take care of their two young sons. Often, he scolds her for neglecting them. Yet, he seems more interested in playing billiards with the men at Klein's Hotel, than in spending time with his family. He is regarded very highly by all the people vacationing on the island. They think he is a perfect husband. Increasingly puzzled by his wife's refusal to play the role he has assigned to her, he goes for help to the family doctor. Leonce is critical of Edna, angry at her decision to stop the entertaining that is required of her, and shocked and embarrassed when she moves out of his house into a small house of her own. He makes up a story in order to preserve appearances that Edna has had to leave because the house they shared is being remodeled. Leonce is incapable of understanding Edna or any woman who does not fit the mold. He is far from a villain, or a brutish lout. He is just not able to accept the changes in his wife.

RAOUL AND ETIENNE PONTELLIER

Edna and Leonce's sons are not three-dimensional characters. We do not see the little boys often, but when they do appear, they always want something. Their nurse takes care of their physical needs, and Edna is not burdened unduly with them. They seem quite independent of their mother, and actually do not rush to her even when they hurt themselves. It is difficult to distinguish Raoul from Etienne. They are always together and they seem to demand something from their mother whenever they do appear. Sometimes they go to visit their paternal grandmother, where they are filled with Creole lore.

EDNA'S FATHER, THE COLONEL

The Colonel is another example of the conventional male, unable to accept a woman who is seeking independence. Although he opposed Edna's marriage to a Catholic, he seems to have accepted this by the time of his visit to New Orleans. He advises his son-in-law to be firm with Edna. His other daughters are excellent wives. He has no understanding of Edna and is quite unsympathetic to her. He was a stern, unloving father when she was growing up, and he presided over a dour household.

ROBERT LEBRUN

A rather callow Creole youth, Robert spends his summers flirting with married women, is not very successful in business, and is always planning to go to Mexico. He acts as a catalyst in stirring Edna's emotions, but he, himself, is really quite ordinary, and in time, Edna begins to understand this. He does, however, have the exoticism of the Creole male, has been raised on mystical tales, and is able to impart some of this to Edna, who responds to Robert's tales of spirits and ghosts.

VICTOR LEBRUN

Robert's younger brother is described as hotheaded and violent, but greatly beloved by his mother. He is spoiled and pampered, but at one point in the story, Edna feels herself suddenly aware of his physical beauty. He seems to be the very incarnation of desire.

MADAME LEBRUN

The owner of a summer resort on Grand Isle, Madame Lebrun is a very busy, efficient woman. Her petticoats are starched; she dresses in white. Although her husband either died or deserted her and their two small children (his whereabouts are somewhat vague), Mme Lebrun seems to have managed quite well. She has a persistent suitor, M. Montel, who has been pursuing her for twenty years.

ADELE RATIGNOLLE

The embodiment of the "mother-woman," Adele Ratignolle is beautiful, plump, golden-haired, completely feminine, and utterly possessed by her motherhood. All her thoughts, plans, desires center around her children. She is pregnant this summer; she seems to be always pregnant, is constantly sewing little garments for her children, both born and unborn, and is a direct contrast to Edna Pontellier. Chopin uses her as a foil to show how different most women are from Edna. She becomes Edna's confidante, but is incapable of understanding a woman like Edna. When she flirts with a young, unattached man, she understands the rules that govern this game, and would never make the mistake of taking him too seriously.

ALCEE AROBIN

Handsome, arrogant, well-known in New Orleans for his scandalous affairs with women, Alcee Arobin is the consummate roue. He knows himself, and he thinks he knows women. He consciously and deliberately sets out to seduce Edna. Obviously, he thinks she is seducible. He is a contrast to Robert, who is far more innocent and is capable of feeling love for a woman. Alcee seems to only feel desire. When he kisses Edna for the first time, Edna responds to him sexually in a way she has never done before.

MADEMOISELLE REISZ

An ugly woman, an immensely talented musician, Mademoiselle Reisz is an example of the independent woman. Her art comes first; she is blunt, outspoken, and recognizes in Edna a spirit that responds passionately to music. She does not feel that Edna has it within her to be an artist because she is not willing to make the necessary sacrifices that art demands. She gets letters from Robert Lebrun when he goes to Mexico and shows them to Edna; she encourages the younger woman in her struggle to become independent. Her apartment becomes a refuge for Edna.

DOCTOR MANDELET

Doctor Mandelet is a kindly, wise man to whom Leonce goes for advice on how to handle Edna, who is becoming increasingly difficult to understand. The doctor assures Leonce that her restlessness will pass and that women are strange creatures, not at all like men. They are willful, capricious, and need a strong hand. When Leonce complains that Edna has gotten some notions in her head concerning the eternal rights of women, and has actually moved out of his bed, the doctor suspects that Edna has been associating with "pseudointellectual women" who have been influencing her. He tells Leonce to let Edna alone and the mood will pass. But the thought does occur to him that there might be another man. He does not voice this though, because "he knew his Creole too well to make such a blunder as that."

MARIEQUITA

This earthy, peasant Spanish girl flirts with the Lebrun brothers and perhaps has been intimate with one or both. She is immediately antagonistic to Edna when Robert takes Edna to mass on Cheniere, the island where the religious service takes place. She understands that Edna's marriage is no deterrent to a passionate affair, nor are the two children. The detail the author gives of the "sand and slime" between Mariequita's toes symbolizes the animalism of the girl. She speaks in Spanish to Robert, who understands her. No one else on the boat going to Cheniere knows what she is saying. A connection is made between Robert and Mariequita. They speak the same language, metaphorically as well as literally.

THE AWAKENING

CRITICAL RECEPTION OF THE AWAKENING

GENERAL CONDEMNATION: 1899

Per Seyersted, a professor of American literature at the University of Oslo, has written what, so far, is the definitive biography of Kate Chopin. While he was in the United States on a fellowship, he had access to stories, letters, and a diary that had not been made public, and in 1969, he published *Kate Chopin, a Critical Biography*. That same year, he edited *The Complete Works of Kate Chopin*, published by Louisiana State University Press. Father Daniel Rankin, Kate Chopin's first biographer, a man who published a biography of the writer in 1932 that has been out of print for many years, was also enormously helpful to Seyersted.

Seyersted's biography carefully traces the critical reception accorded *The Awakening*. Chopin's controversial novel was published on April 22, 1899 to general condemnation. Frances Porcher, writing in the *Mirror*, a local newspaper in St. Louis, said that Edna should have been satisfied with her marriage since Leonce gave her everything, including freedom. She was very critical of the heroine since it was not love that awakened her, but sensual passion. Porcher added, rather wistfully, that she wished Chopin had not written the novel. Porcher complained about what an "ugly, cruel, loathsome monster Passion can be when, like a tiger, it slowly stretches its graceful length and yawns and finally awakens." She added that the book leaves "one sick of human nature."

Two St. Louis newspapers agreed with the *Mirror*. *The Globe Democrat* called it morbid because the author had failed to teach a moral lesson. *The Republic* said it was "too strong drink for moral babes, and should be labeled poison."

"Sad, Mad, Bad." C.L. Deyo's review in the *St. Louis Post-Dispatch*, was kinder, praising the mastery with which the difficult subject was treated, but added that the novel "is sad and mad and bad, but it is all consummate art." Alexander De Menil, a member of the St. Louis literary world, refused to review the book in his magazine. There was a general outcry, and the book was banned by the St. Louis libraries. Chopin found herself rejected by old acquaintances, and was refused membership in the St. Louis Fine Arts Club.

She wrote a rejoinder in the August issue of *Book-News*.

Having a group of people at my disposal, I thought it might be entertaining (to myself) to throw them together and see what would happen. I never dreamed of Mrs. Pontellier making such a mess of things and working out her own damnation as she did. If I had the slightest intimation of such a thing I would have excluded her from the company. But when I found out what she was up to, the play was half over and it was too late.

CHOPIN'S DISINGENUOUS DISCLAIMER

Amusing as this statement is, it is hard to believe that Chopin, a careful, meticulous craftsman, would allow a character to take over. Her comment about Edna making a "mess of things," sounds quite disingenuous. Edna certainly did more than make a mess. Did Chopin really see her character as "working out her damnation?" Most readers think that Edna worked out her salvation. Seyersted writes that this statement represents "minor concessions to the public." No modern reader can take Chopin's disclaimer seriously.

Subsequent criticism continued to be mixed. The book was described as a "brilliant piece of writing" by one critic, but *The New Orleans Times-Democrat* complained "The real Mrs. Chopin ... is at her best as a creator of sweet and lovable characters." The *Chicago Times Herald* declared that "It was not necessary for a writer of so great refinement and poetic grace to enter the overworked field of sex fiction."

Chopin was deeply hurt at the reception of her book. She refused to discuss the subject with anyone, wrote little after this blow, and died in 1904, just five years after the publication of *The Awakening*.

SHOCK: 1909

Percival Pollard, in 1909, tongue firmly in cheek, wrote an essay called "The Unlikely Awakening of a Married Woman", expressing exaggerated shock at the passionate awakenings of young married women and the heat these awakenings cause. "Of course, she went and drowned herself. She realized that you can only put out fire with water."

Father Rankin, Chopin's first biographer, wrote in 1932 that he considered *The Awakening* morbid in **theme**. He felt that her strength was as a regional writer, and she should have directed her considerable talents in that direction. In 1953, Cryrille Arnavon translated the novel into French and wrote an introduction that praised Mrs. Chopin's courageous realism."

FIRST-RATE IMPRESSIONISM: 1956

Kenneth Eble, in 1956, commended the work as first-rate in an article that was later used as an introduction to a 1964 reprint of the novel. He also said "quite frankly, the book is about sex." but added that the way "scene, mood, action and character are fused reminds one not so much of literature, as of an impressionist painting, of a Renoir, with much of the sweetness missing."

Among the critics who have reevaluated the book favorably in recent years are Edmund Wilson, Lewis Leary, Van Wyck Brooks, and of course, Per Seyersted.

Edmund Wilson, in 1962, writing in his widely acclaimed masterpiece *Patriotic Gore*, a study of the literature of the American Civil War, praised Chopin's book warmly. "… quite uninhibited and beautifully written, which anticipates D.H. Lawrence in its treatment of infidelity." Van Wyck Brooks called it "a small, perfect book that mattered more than the whole life work of many a prolific writer."

Lewis Leary, the editor of the 1970 edition of *The Awakening and Other Stories by Kate Chopin*, wrote that Mrs. Chopin has depicted a trapped and desperate woman, who embarks on a drama of self-discovery, of "a tragedy perhaps of self-deceit … Her awakening, only vaguely intellectual, is disturbingly physical." He places her among other fictional heroines who have searched for freedom and failed. He mentions Nathaniel Hawthorne's Hester Prynne, Gustave Flaubert's Emma Bovary, and Henry James' Isabel Archer.

PASSION AS A SUBJECT FOR FICTION

Seyersted claims that Kate Chopin's great achievement was that she was "the first woman writer in her country to accept passion as a legitimate subject for serious, outspoken fiction." He says that it is probably difficult for a modern reader to understand how brave and honest she was. "She was something of a pioneer in the amoral treatment of sexuality, of divorce, and of woman's urge for an existential authenticity. She is, in many respects, a modern writer, particularly in her awareness of the complexities of truth and the complications of freedom."

FATAL COMPROMISE?

In 1970, George Spangler differed from the positive comments on the novel in an essay called "Kate Chopin's *The Awakening*: A Partial Dissent." He finds fault with the ending, saying that Edna's characterization is inconsistent here, and the reader is asked to accept a different and diminished Edna. Her determination and strength are shown throughout the book and her death, this critic says, does not suit this kind of strong woman. Her sudden collapse does not run true to what has been shown before. This is not a woman who would die from "disappointed, illicit love." Chopin wrote this ending to satisfy her readers' moralistic demands. "Edna has sinned in thought and deed against accepted sexual morality, and for the average reader in 1899, her sin required that she suffer and die."

Spangler adds that Chopin's attempt to pacify her public didn't work, for the book created a scandal, and the ending reduces Edna's character.

CHOPIN'S PRESCIENCE

Feminists in the 1960s and 1970s were amazed when they saw the original publication date of *The Awakening*. Linda Wolfe, writing in *The New York Times*, said the book "speaks to me as pertinently as any fiction published this year or last. It is uncanny, ... a Masterpiece." Jean Stafford, writing in *The New York Review of Books*, said that "Kate Chopin was long before her time in dealing with sexual passion ... and the personal emotions of women." Many other readers couldn't believe the original publication date. How could a woman writing in 1899 be so prescient? Many found themselves checking the date of publication again and again, in genuine astonishment. In 1906, it had been reprinted by Duffield but had the gone out of print for over fifty years. How extraordinary a find this was for all readers, not only the feminist critics!

A FREUDIAN GLOSS

Cynthia Griffin Wolff added a Freudian interpretation in 1973 in an essay called "Thanatos and Eros; Kate Chopin's *The Awakening*." She comments on Edna's interest in food as evidence of her infantile nature. Wolff feels that Edna is arrested at a pregenital level and that her appetites are "fixated at the oral level." She is unable to have a mature sexual relationship with a man because of this fixation. "A genital relationship, like all ego-relationships, necessarily involves limitations; to put the matter in Edna's terms, a significant attachment with a real man would involve relinquishing the fantasy of total fulfillment with some fantasy lover."

Ms. Wolff also refers to the myth of the sleeping beauty. As we have seen, Edna spends a lot of time sleeping. She even goes to sleep while on an outing with Robert Lebrun. When she awakens, she asks Robert how long she has slept. She says that everything seems to have changed. Robert jokingly says that she has slept precisely one hundred years. Wolff compares the sleeping beauty's awakening to Edna's. The fairy tale princess is awakened with a kiss, to love; Edna wakes up, without a kiss, to physical hunger and to food. Wolff uses this as proof that Edna is arrested at a pregenital, oral stage.

EDNA, A TIMELESS CREATION

In this brief survey of the critical reception accorded *The Awakening*, we can see not only how the response to a work of art has changed in the century since the book appeared, but also how society has changed. A book that caused a scandal in 1899 in St. Louis has been reevaluated today, and is no longer scandalous at all. What is remarkable about *The Awakening* today is that it was out of print for so many years because of puritanical attitudes; that it was written by Kate Chopin, a woman who was certainly a product of her repressive time; and that it still has something to say, even to modern readers, who may take a woman's sensual nature for granted. The book still yields pleasure, especially to a reader accustomed to graphic depictions of sexual acts. In Chopin's restraint, there is more sensuality than in many modern works of sexual acrobatics. She was able to evoke a wonderful sense of place, to use her skills as a colorist to sketch the Creole society of the time, and to create a character in Edna, who struggled with many of the issues that modern women are still wrestling with: sexuality, maternity, marriage, work, privacy, fantasy, individuality.

CHOPIN COMPARED WITH JAMES, FLAUBERT, MILLER

COMPARISON WITH PORTRAIT OF A LADY BY HENRY JAMES

Isabel Archer, beautiful, brilliant, intelligent, surprised by a substantial inheritance left to her by her uncle, pursued by three eligible men, is tricked into marrying a man who hates her, and who is after her money. After discovering the true nature of her husband, she chooses, perhaps perversely, perhaps out of embarrassment at admitting her mistake, perhaps out of pride, or a desire for martyrdom, to remain in a marriage that is a horror.

Masterpieces major and minor

In comparing *Portrait of a Lady* to *The Awakening*, one realizes immediately the difference between a major masterpiece and a minor one. Isabel's character is fully developed; the reader knows her background, her ambitions, her thoughts, her desires and her perversity, which help her choose the wrong man, and then insist on keeping him. Edna is more one-dimensional. We do not enter often into her thoughts; perhaps because she is a less intelligent heroine, more intuitive, responding instinctively to her newly awakened passions. Isabel is more cerebral, and she seems less aware of her sensuality (maybe because she is a Jamesian heroine, none of whom is noted for passions of the body). In one of the last chapters of the book, when Caspar Goodwood, an American, in love with her for years, kisses her passionately, Isabel is terrified of losing herself in this man's embrace. She resists what Caspar offers her, and chooses to remain in a sterile, hateful marriage.

Somehow this satisfies her desire for suffering and for the grandeur she seems to feel such pain will bring her. She cannot bring herself to admit how stirred she was by Goodwood's embrace.

Edna, the less intellectual character, understands her own nature better. She knows, by the end of the novel, just what she is, and what she needs. Her decision to kill herself is an act of independence, while Isabel's decision to remain in her marriage seems to be an act that does not stem from an understanding and acceptance of her own nature. It can be seen as an act of pride, or stubbornness, a refusal to admit a mistake. Isabel cannot accept her sexuality, and perhaps by remaining in a loveless marriage, she can continue her pretense.

Both books depict unhappy marriages. Isabel is married to a demonic man, while Edna is married to merely an insensitive, acquisitive one, not too different, it is clearly indicated, from most of the men of this society.

Although Isabel doesn't physically die at the end of *Portrait of a Lady*, her renunciation of love and passion and her decision to remain with her husband do constitute a death of the spirit. The reader feels more pained at Isabel's end than at Edna's death. It seems ironic that Edna, the less intellectual character, is the one who achieves self-knowledge, while Isabel, a far superior character, in terms of intelligence, depth, sensitivity, integrity, is unable to accept that part of herself, her sensuality, and condemns herself to what the reader can only perceive as a lifetime of suffering. Martyrdom is what Isabel wants.

COMPARISON WITH MADAME BOVARY BY GUSTAVE FLAUBERT

To compare *The Awakening* to *Madame Bovary* is to compare a flute solo to an orchestral arrangement. *Madame Bovary* is a major work, encompassing not only extraordinary characterization, a thorough study of the deadliness of provincial life, but also an attack on an excess of romantic sensibility. When Flaubert said, "Madame Bovary, C'est moi," he expressed not only his identification with his heroine, but also how much of his life was in this book, which took him five years to write. His niece Caroline described how as a child she thought that the word "Bovary," meant work, because her uncle would always say, with a sigh, "It's time now to return to Bovary," and she imagined that meant it was time to go to work. He wrote very slowly, always looking for just the right word, the perfect phrase. He spent all night at work and then produced almost nothing. In five days, he had finished only one page. At another time he was able to write only twenty pages in a month, although he worked more than seven hours every day. Flaubert documented his artistic struggles in many complaining letters to his mistress, Louise Colet, a fellow writer, who commiserated with him, but urged him to come and visit her, which he resisted. "I lead a bitter kind of life, devoid of all external joy, where I've nothing to sustain me except a kind of permanent rage, which shrieks out sometimes with impotence, which is continuous. Yet I love my work, with a frenzied and perverted love, as the ascetic loves the hair-shirt which scratches his belly."

Kate Chopin did not labor in this frenzied way over *The Awakening*. Per Seyersted, her biographer, said that she wrote only for a few hours, in the morning, two or three days a week. She did not like to rewrite, and was a very social creature, enjoying card parties, concerts, and visits with friends. Of course, Chopin was a widow and the mother of six children, while Flaubert never married and was able to devote himself totally to writing, due to what has been called a fortunate disposition to epilepsy. Because he was an invalid, and his doting mother had enough money to support them both, Flaubert's entire life revolved around his writing. Chopin's writing seems to have been only a part, albeit a very important part, of a more normal life. Flaubert's total dedication yielded a masterpiece, while Chopin's partial dedication resulted in what might be called a fine, minor work. Nevertheless, there are many similarities in the two books.

Flaubert issued, then awarded a medal

Madame Bovary created a scandal when it was published in 1856. In fact, St. Beuve, famous critic and writer, wrote, "You know everything, Monsieur, but you're cruel." The critics complained that there is not one person who is good or kind or noble in the book. Flaubert's fame, or notoriety, was firmly established with the public trial in 1857. He was accused of writing a scandalous book that was offensive and against public morals and religion. His publisher and printer were also accused of offenses against morality. The defendants were all acquitted, but they were reprimanded for "presenting a picture of the delinquencies which may exist in society," and the judge did not award them costs.

Flaubert was quite sure of himself. "I don't care a jot if my novel annoys the bourgeois. I don't care a jot if they take us to the courts." He lived for thirteen years after the trial, enjoying a great measure of success, and he was finally awarded the Medal of Honor.

Chopin's book also created a scandal, but it was not as public a scandal, perhaps because she was only a woman writer, and it wasn't necessary to make such a fuss about a mere woman who had the temerity to write such a shocking book. Maybe if she had the public airing of a trial such as Flaubert suffered, or enjoyed, Chopin might have fared better. Instead, snipings by critics, shunning by society, betrayals by friends, caused the author to retreat from the world she knew, and she never wrote anything of significance after the furor caused by *The Awakening*. She did not openly protest her accusers, but she did write a disclaimer saying that her characters had gotten away from her, and she was not in control. How much more noble was Flaubert's "I don't give a jot!" In spite of Chopin's independence and feminism, she was unable to resist the scurrilous attacks against her and succumbed to what Flaubert would have called "bourgeois morality."

Emma and Edna compared

In many ways the two main characters are alike, but they are also different. Both Emma and Edna are victims of an excess of romantic tendencies. They both idealize their lovers, and then are bitterly disappointed. Emma has read quantities of romantic literature, which has completely distorted her thinking, and she enjoyed the mysticism of her convent education and the romanticism of Catholicism. In fact she even invented sins when she went to confession when she was a young girl. Edna finds herself in a Catholic milieu in the Creole society she married into, and is enchanted by the myths and exotic stories Robert Lebrun tells her. She is shocked and puzzled by the easy sexuality of the Catholic women, and by their acceptance of their femininity and their roles in society. She had been brought up in an atmosphere of dour Presbyterianism, and the mysticism of her husband's religion confuses her, but seems to excite her.

Both Emma and Edna are bored with their husbands. They both neglect their households and their children. Emma has little interest in her daughter, and Edna is described as being very different from the other women who are called "mother-women." Emma is cruel to her daughter. Edna is indifferent to her sons.

Emma becomes infatuated with Leon. She romanticizes their relationship, and when he leaves for Paris, she is easily seduced by a cad, Rodolphe, Edna is infatuated with Robert Lebrun, who becomes frightened when their flirtation turns serious and who runs away to Mexico. Alcee Arobin, a well-known roue, seduces her. Both women exhibit little remorse after their first adulterous liaison.

The husbands compared

Charles, Emma's husband, whom many readers see as the only good person in the book, is patient, bovine, long-suffering, boring, incompetent as a doctor, but passionately in love with Emma. Sometimes he cannot keep his hands or eyes off her. He annoys Emma, and she is cruel to him. Leonce, Edna's husband, is successful, popular, wealthy, discriminating, but humorless. He seems conventionally attached to Edna, but more attached to his creature comforts and to making a certain kind of appearance. He doesn't seem capable of much passion, but he is not a brute. He is concerned about Edna, and seeks help from the family doctor. Neither husband is a villain, and Charles evokes considerable sympathy from the reader for his dumb patience and love for his ungrateful wife.

Emma longs for elegance, beauty, excitement, romance, passion. When she goes to a ball she sees, for the first time, the life she would like to lead. This visit is a turning point for her, and she is never the same after. The description of the dinner at Vaubyessard is similar in many details to the dinner that Edna gives before she moves to her own home. The atmosphere of luxury, paganism, elegance is the same; even the descriptions of the table settings are alike: the candles, the cloth, the flowers. Edna's dinner also marks a turning point. She is leaving her husband's home. The celebration she plans (at her husband's expense) marks a significant change in her life and is symbolic of her attempts at independence.

Emma has been called the ultimate consumer, possessed by longings for material things, dresses, shawls, bonnets, capes, whereas Edna is not interested at all in these things. Perhaps because she has always had them, she doesn't care at all for possessions. Actually, when she moves to the pigeon house, she strips herself of most of her things, wanting only the basic necessities. Emma's downfall comes about as a result of her excessive materialism, which leads her into disastrous debts. Edna wants freedom for herself, and to be able to do what she wants. Their suicides are very different. Emma takes arsenic, and dies a long, painful, undignified death, while Edna decides to swim out further than any woman has done before. Her death comes in a very conscious, almost elegant manner. Her strokes taking her to her death are long and easy, not frantic at all. Emma dies in a hysterical fashion. Edna dies quietly.

Symbolic figures

Both books use symbolic figures in the background, which appear almost as a **refrain**. In Madame Bovary, a blind beggar appears as a portent of doom, death, disease, insanity, ruin. As Emma moves closer to calamity, this figure is seen more frequently. In *The Awakening*, the lady in black, always following the figures of the lovers, reappears as a symbol of death, a warning of what happens to lovers in this world.

Flaubert has been criticized for his constantly shifting narrative viewpoint. He starts out with a first person narrator, then switches to an omniscient one, and the identity of the first narrator is never clear. Eventually the viewpoint of the narrator becomes Emma's, but not before the narrator makes many satiric comments about the middle class. It has been pointed out that it would have been too limiting to restrict the point of view to Emma herself, since she really isn't too bright or perceptive, and Flaubert had to avail himself of other narrative voices. In *The Awakening*, Chopin does use Edna's point of view a great deal of the time, although she also allows for narrative intrusions.

In an introduction to the Signet edition of *Madame Bovary* in 1964, Mary McCarthy wrote that Emma is not a tragic figure. Instead she is pathetic, because she is so ordinary and trite. McCarthy compared Tolstoy's *Anna Karenina* to Emma and found Anna tragic because of the nobility of her passion. There is nothing noble about Emma. She is a vain, selfish, cruel, foolish woman. Edna has perhaps more nobility about her. She wanted more out of life than furbelows and trimmings. She wanted passion, independence, and as she put it, "my own way." There is something grand about that aspiration.

COMPARISON WITH THE GOOD MOTHER BY SUE MILLER

In 1986 Sue Miller wrote her first novel, *The Good Mother*. In it she explored the conflict between a woman's newly awakened sexuality, and her passionate love for her child. There are many similarities between Edna Pontellier, the **protagonist** of Chopin's *The Awakening*, and Anna Dunlap, the main character in Miller's *The Good Mother*. There is also one great dissimilarity.

Both Anna and Edna are second-rate artists; Anna is a pianist who realizes as a young girl that she is not good enough. Her family, with painfully high aspirations for all the children, is obviously disappointed. Anna gives piano lessons, but never deludes herself into thinking that she is a fine musician. Edna is a dilettante artist, dabbling in art, establishing a studio, demanding that people pose for her, but also understanding that she does not have the passion nor the talent to be a truly fine artist. Both women are honest in their self-assessments of their artistic talents.

Inhibited marriages

Both women have had repressed marriages. Anna never awoke sexually while living with her husband. He was too much like her: too prudish, too rigid. He could not free her, turn her into the passionate woman she longed to be. When Anna realized, as a young girl, that she could never fulfill the hopes of her family, especially her grandfather, of becoming a fine musician, she turned to promiscuous sex with a number of boys, who used her, and then talked about how "easy" she was. She never experienced orgasm with any of these casual sexual encounters. Nor did she with her husband, an earnest, stuffy lawyer. Edna also was unawakened by her husband. She had three early infatuations, as a young girl, but they were never even acknowledged, let alone consummated. Of course, the period of time of *The Awakening* is completely different, and casual premarital sex was certainly not common when Chopin was writing. Nevertheless, Edna seems remarkably innocent and unaware of sexual passion.

Both women are awakened sexually. Anna has a tumultuous love affair with Leo, an artist. He turns her into what she always wanted to be-a passionate, orgasmic woman. Miller is quite graphic in her sexual descriptions, reflecting the era in which she is writing, but it is interesting to note that both Chopin and Miller use some of the same images to show their characters becoming aware of their own bodies. Anna looks at the texture of her own skin as if she has never seen it before, and Edna looks at her white, plump arm, as if she were seeing it for the first time. The descriptions of Edna's seduction by Alcee Arobin, a well-known womanizer, although certainly very discreet by our standards today, were considered shocking in 1899 when Chopin wrote. Her use of sexual **imagery** also caused her book to fall into disfavor, so for her time, Chopin would have been considered as graphic as Miller is today.

When Anna and her husband agree to a rather amicable divorce, Anna refuses to take money from him, except for her daughter Molly's support. She wants to be independent and self-sufficient, and sees her husband's money as keeping her from both. She also refuses her grandfather's offer of help, and chooses to live in a shabby apartment, near railroad, where she can support herself by giving piano lessons and working part-time in a laboratory testing rats. She sees her ability to support herself and her child as crucial to her development as a grown-up. Edna wants to live alone and support herself without her husband's largess. She also moves into a modest house, supporting herself through a small inheritance, her winnings at the race track, and by selling some of her sketches. Both these characters recognize the importance of what Virginia

Woolf called *A Room of One's Own*. Having their own money is essential to both.

Both women have friends who are alike. Mademoiselle Reisz, an independent, talented musician becomes Edna's confidante. She offers her a refuge in her apartment, and acts as an intermediary between Edna and Robert Lebrun, the young man with whom Edna is infatuated. She tells Edna about the demands of being an artist, and plays for her so beautifully that Edna is often moved to tears. Mademoiselle Reisz is a difficult woman, nonconventional, demanding, but very fond of Edna, and recognizes in her a sensitivity that is rare. She doesn't hesitate to be honest with Edna, and points out to her how ordinary a man Robert is. In spite of the differences in age, upbringing, attitudes, the two women become good friends. Ursula, in *The Good Mother* is also a nonconventional character. Anna gives Ursula piano lessons, shares with her new friend her pain and terror at the possible loss of her child. Ursula responds by offering her pills to dull the pain, pizza to fill the hunger, and tells her what no one else has. "Everyone knows you're a good mother." The modern character does all in her power to comfort her friend, shares sexual secrets, provides some comic relief, and is as flamboyant a figure as Mademoiselle Reisz is in *The Awakening*. It is also interesting to see how friendships have changed through the years. Mlle Reisz offers music, conversation, a refuge, advice, wisdom. Ursala offers drugs, food, her own history of sexual indiscretions, as comfort. Yet the sincerity of both women is genuine, and their desire to aid and comfort their friends is very similar.

Lovers who make mistakes

Anna falls in love with a man who makes a serious mistake. He allows Molly, Anna's three-year-old daughter, to touch his genitals when she sees him undressed. Thinking that Anna's casual freedom with nudity and the body is appropriate, he makes the mistake that will bring anguish to all of them. Molly tells her father about the incident when she visits him, and the father sues for custody, claiming that Anna is an unfit mother. Leo did not molest the child in any way, but he used bad judgment, and because of it, Anna's feelings toward him change irrevocably.

Edna falls in love with Robert Lebrun, who also uses bad judgment. He has flirted with many Creole women in the summertime, but this time, he flirts with Edna, not a Creole and not accustomed to the flirtatious games played in this society by young men and married women. He also brings tragedy to everyone involved. He doesn't understand Edna, and he becomes frightened by her passion, and leaves her. After he runs away to Mexico, she is easily seduced by Alcee, a man given to such activities.

How Edna and Anna differ

The great dissimilarity between Edna and Anna is in their feelings for their children. Edna is not a "mother-woman." She is detached from her children, except for one brief visit, where she visits them at their grandmother's home and seems very loving and maternal. Chopin uses the same sensual descriptions of maternal love in this chapter of her book that Miller does. Both women look at their children hungrily; they savor the texture of the children's skin, the smell of their bodies. Anna is always filled with this passionate love; Edna has these sensations momentarily, and they leave her quickly, when she returns to her own home. Anna is indeed *The Good Mother* of the title, but she allows her erotic need to becloud her judgment. Because of this she loses her child, and this loss completely destroys the passion she had felt for Leo, the man who awakened her. There is no question where Anna's loyalties will lie, once she understands that she may lose her child. She is willing to give up Leo. She would do anything to save her child. Edna's desire for independence and freedom is the most important thing in her life, more important even than her children. She will not sacrifice this newfound part of herself even for her children, she says. When she realizes that the kind of independence she wants, including sexual independence, cannot be reconciled with marriage and motherhood, she decides to destroy herself. For Anna, life without Molly is unbearable. For Edna, life without freedom is unbearable.

THE AWAKENING

ESSAY QUESTIONS AND ANSWERS

Question: Compare Adele Ratignolle To Edna Pontellier.

Answer: Adele Ratignolle is the perfect example of the "mother-woman." A beautiful, feminine woman whose primary concern is her three children, she is pregnant again during this summer that she spends on Grand Isle. Unhappy at being parted from her children, even for a little while, she is always sewing something for them. Children's undergarments and drawers can fascinate her and provide a topic for conversation. She understands the flirtatious games played in this Creole society and knows how to fend off amorous advances made by young unmarried males, but she can still enjoy the sparring. She is utterly comfortable and fulfilled in her role as wife and mother.

Edna Pontellier is the exact opposite. She is less conventionally beautiful, is described as "handsome," and "noble," and is thinner, and is not consumed by motherhood. She pays perfunctory attention to her two young sons, who do not seem very attached to her. She is relieved when they go away for a visit. She is interested in art. She sketches, and has a natural ability. She is not Creole, was born into a repressive Presbyterian family, and does not know how to play the flirtatious games that married women and single men play on this island. She becomes infatuated with Robert, begins to awaken sexually, wants to free herself from the confines of marriage and motherhood, and is unhappy enough to commit suicide when she realizes she cannot reconcile her own needs with those of her family.

Question: Compare Robert Lebrun To Alcee Arobin.

Answer: Robert Lebrun, an impecunious, charming bachelor, spends his summers on Grand Isle, where his mother owns a pension. He amuses himself by flirting with the married women. He is capable of an innocent flirtation with Edna, but when he feels that matters are getting too serious, he flees to Mexico. He is sensitive, exotic, touched by the magic of the Creole he has grown up with, but is not extraordinary in any way. His teasing attentions stimulate Edna and cause her to awaken from her sleep of repression. He is the catalyst in the story. Weak, impetuous, somewhat foolish, completely incapable of understanding a woman like Edna, Robert should be harmless. It is Edna's response that causes the danger.

Alcee Arobin is dangerous. A well-known roue, irresponsible, reckless, lustful, he quickly senses Edna's state of arousal and takes advantage of it. His kisses stir Edna passionately for the first time in her life. When she allows herself to be seduced by a man she knows she doesn't love, she understands what animal passion is. If Robert had seduced her, she would probably have been able to rationalize it as a culmination of a great love. She cannot delude herself about Alcee Arobin. Robert is responsible for Edna's awakening, but Alcee is partially responsible for Edna's end.

Question: How Is The Setting Of Grand Isle Important In The Development Of The Plot?

Answer: Grand Isle, an island fifty miles off the coast of Louisiana, is a summer resort for the wealthy members of Creole society who winter in New Orleans. Surrounded by the warm water of the Gulf of Mexico, lulled by gentle breezes, filled with the odors of jasmine, the island is Eden-like. And it is here that Edna, like the original inhabitants of the Garden of Eden, eats of the tree of knowledge. Edna, a repressed, discontented society matron, unfulfilled by her marriage and motherhood, is loosened by the sounds, smells, and primitive quality of Grand Isle and indulges in a flirtation. She is deeply stirred by music, learns to swim for the first time in the tepid waters of the Gulf, and under the spell of the setting begins to shed inhibitions. She finds out that she is a passionate animal and this self-knowledge, which she is unable to reconcile with being a wife and mother, results in her death.

Question: Discuss The Role Of A Married Woman In Creole Society Of This Time.

Answer: A married woman, in this Creole society at this time, was very limited. She was Catholic, so that birth control, primitive at best at that time, was forbidden. Therefore, she was pregnant frequently. She was supposed to take care of her children and household, supervise the servants, plan the menus, create a beautiful home, be able to play a musical instrument, perhaps sketch, maybe sing. She must not take any of these artistic accomplishments seriously. They were supposed to enhance the charm of her home and reflect on her husband. A wife was a possession, one to be cared for and displayed. Her needs were to be sublimated and she was supposed to be completely fulfilled by being a wife and mother. She, of course, was not responsible for contributing to the family income through working at a job. She came to the marriage with a dowry, and, perhaps, some inherited wealth.

Question: Discuss The **Theme** Of Man's Inability To Understand Woman.

Answer: That man is incapable of understanding woman is a **theme** in *The Awakening*. Edna's father, a rigid, rather dour man, gave her little affection as a child and did not approve of her marriage because Leonce Pontellier was Catholic. He should have disapproved of Edna's marriage for other reasons: Leonce was twelve years older; Edna was not in love. Once Edna is married, he tells his son-in-law to be firm with her. He is utterly unsympathetic to a daughter or a wife who will not conform. It is mentioned that he hastened his wife's death through coercion.

Leonce regards his wife as a possession. He wants to display her; he wants her to adorn his home; he wants her to take care of the children and keep them from disturbing him. When Edna refuses to entertain the way she had in the past, and shows signs of rebelling, he goes for help to Doctor Mandelet.

Doctor Mandelet tells Leonce that women are moody, high-strung, irritable. They are difficult creatures to manage, but they must be handled. The doctor obviously feels that a woman must be broken, like a high-spirited horse.

Robert Lebrun flirts with Edna, teases her, fills her head with Creole lore, but is incapable of understanding her. He doesn't know what Edna really is; he doesn't really want to know. To Robert, women are enigmatic and exciting, but that's about all he understands. He could not accept Edna's independence, and if she ever married him, they both would be unhappy.

Alcee Arobin doesn't understand Edna either. He doesn't try to. He just wants to seduce her. He sees women as sexual playthings. The chase is what excites him. Not one of the men in this novel understands women: neither father, husband, lover, doctor, nor seducer.

Question: Why Was The Public So Shocked By *The Awakening*?

Answer: *The Awakening* was published in 1899. Readers were shocked to read about a woman who has affairs, moves out of her husband's house, is not terribly interested in her children, wants a career, wants a self. These things were scandalous at the time, years before women got the vote, were able to handle their own finances, and were encouraged to pursue careers. The sensual descriptions of water, the element that serves to awaken Edna, the sensuosity of the island itself, a paradise in which a woman is loosened of habitual restraints, the evocation of lush, unrestrained growth, both of the island and of Edna's passionate nature, caused the book to be taken off the library shelves in St. Louis, where the author was living. She had jeopardized her reputation and her livelihood by writing such a disturbing book.

Question: Discuss The Use Of Bird Symbolism In *The Awakening*.

Answer: From the first screeching of the caged parrot, hung outside the pension on Grand Isle, "Get out! Get out!" the symbolism of a bird in a cage is established. Edna is a bird even though her cage is gilded. She is confined by marriage and motherhood. She is described as having "quick, bright eyes." There is something bird-like about her appearance. The cry of "Get out! Get out!" is heard again in the novel and symbolizes what Edna is trying to do.

When Edna moves out of her husband's home into a tiny place of her own, her new shelter is called "the pigeon house." Pigeons are not caged; they are free to come and go, unlike the parrot who has been tamed and domesticized. Edna views the pigeon house as a place where she can be free of her habitual constraints. It is where she will taste freedom.

BIBLIOGRAPHY

WORKS OF KATE CHOPIN

Seyersted, Per, Ed. *The Complete Works of Kate Chopin*. Two Volumes. Baton Rouge: Louisiana State University Press, 1969.

BIOGRAPHIES OF KATE CHOPIN

Deyo, C. L. "Mrs. Kate Chopin." *St. Louis Life*, IX (June 9, 1894), 11–12.

Rankin, Daniel S. *Kate Chopin and Her Creole Stories*. Philadelphia: University of Pennsylvania Press, 1932.

Seyersted, Per. *Kate Chopin: A Critical Biography*. Baton Rouge: Louisiana State University Press, 1969.

BIBLIOGRAPHY

Potter, Richard H. "Kate Chopin and Her Critics: An Annotated Checklist." *The Bulletin-Missouri Historical Society*, XXVI (July 1970), 306–17.

CRITICISM

Arnavon, Cyrille. "Les Debuts du Roman Realiste Americain et L'Influence Francaise," In: *Romanciers Americains Contemporains*. Henri Kerst, Ed. Paris: Cahiers des Langues Modernes, 1946, 9–35.

Brooks, Van Wyck. *The Confident Years*: 1885–1915. New York: 1952, 341.

Eble, Kenneth. "A Forgotten Novel: Kate Chopin's Awakening," *Western Humanities Review*, X (Summer 1956), 261–269.

Leary, Lewis. *Southern Excursion: Essays on Mark Twain and Others*. Baton Rouge: Louisiana State University Press, 1971, 169–74.

_____ "Introduction," *The Awakening and Other Stories*. New York: Holt, Rinehart and Winston, Inc., 1970.

_____ "Kate Chopin and Walt Whitman," *Walt Whitman Review*, XVI (December 1970), 120–21.

Pollard, Percival. *Their Day in Court*. New York and Washington: Neale Publishing, 1909, 41–45.

Seyersted, Per. *Kate Chopin: A Critical Biography*. Baton Rouge: Louisiana State University Press, 1969.

Spangler, George. "Kate Chopin's *The Awakening*: A Partial Dissent." *Novel*, III (Spring, 1970), 249–55.

Wilson, Edmund. *Patriotic Gore: Studies in the Literature of the American Civil War*. New York: Oxford University Press, 1962, 587–593.

Wolff, Cynthia Griffin. "Thanatos and Eros: Kate Chopin's *The Awakening*." *American Quarterly*, XXV (Oct, 1973), 449–71.